★ Basic Dialogue

★ Reading Zone

★ Listening Zone

★ Grammar & Writing Zone

★ Let's Play (Activity Page)

★ Let's Do It At Home (Homework)

★ Writing Practice Page

★ Evaluation Exam

KB249647

Jump

Get Ready

3

Author Samuel Lee | Chanam Kim

Editorial Supervisor LLS English Research Center

J PLUS
Language Publishing Co.

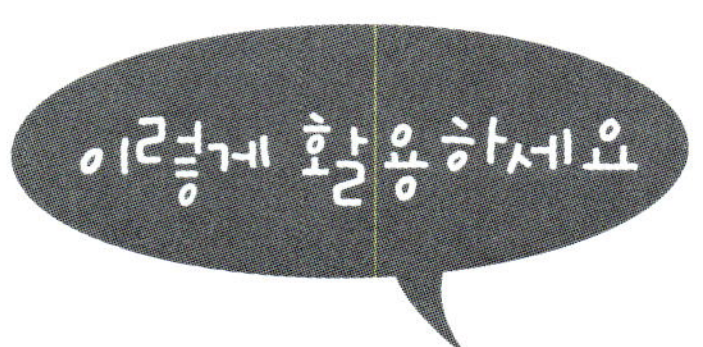

Tips

1) Time allotment 1회 50분 수업의 알찬 진행을 위해 매 페이지마다 수업 진행시간이 표기되어 있습니다.
2) Writing Practice Pages(Express Yourself): 매 과의 중심 단어와 표현을 써 볼 수 있는 페이지입니다.
3) Evaluation Exam: 각 8과씩 공부한 후 중간 학습 평가 시험을, 최종 Final Test를 통해 학생들의 실력을 평가할 수 있습니다.
4) Audio Script: 웹사이트에서 모든 과의 대화와 리스닝 문제를 다운 받아 사용하실 수 있습니다.

각 과의 구성

1) Dialogue: 주요 표현들과 대화 구문들로 구성하였습니다. 롤플레이로 본문 속 주인공들이 되어 재미있게 말해 보세요.
2) Reading Zone: 대화를 통해 알게 된 본문의 내용을 비교적 쉬운 구문으로 다시 재정리하여 구성한 본격적인 Reading 수업용 이야기입니다. 대화체보다는 조금 더 길어진 문장들을 또박또박 읽고 제시된 질문들에 답변하면서 다시 한번 본문의 내용을 꼼꼼히 살펴 보세요.
3) Listening Zone: 문제를 듣고 풀면서 배운 내용들을 확인해 보세요.
4) Grammar & Writing Zone: 그 과를 통해서 꼭 정리해야 할 기본적이고 필수적인 영어 문법을 배우고 배운 문법을 잘 활용하도록 패턴화된 Writing 연습을 통해 익히도록 합니다.
5) Let's Play: 여러 재미있는 액티비티를 통해 그 과에서 배운 내용을 다양한 방법으로 말해보며 복습해 보세요.
6) Let's Do It At Home: 숙제를 하거나 수업시간에 복습용으로 활용하세요.

Get Ready Jump

Samuel Lee

Hello and welcome to the Get Ready Jump series of books!

This thoughtful series will give children a fun and interactive means of learning English.

The wonderful illustrations will engage youngsters whilst exposing them to foreign cultures and teach them about grammar usage.

Of course there is the requisite balanced exploration of the 4 main arenas in studying English: speaking, listening, writing and reading.

But the Get Ready Jump series of books endeavors to enrich the lives of children by making learning a joyful experience.

Chanam Kim

"Get Ready Jump 3은 이전의 Get Ready Jump 2와 마찬가지로 어린이들이 일상 생활에서 접할 수 있는 다양한 상황들을 통하여 자신이 표현하고 싶었던 내용들을 역할극이나 노래, 게임 등을 통해 자연스럽고 재미있게 습득하도록 구성되었습니다.

본 Get Ready Jump 3는 2권에 이어 체계적인 영어 구문 학습을 위한 "Reading Zone"과 "Grammar & Writing Zone"을 강화하고 영어 학습의 각 주요 영역들을 세분화하여 좀 더 짜임새 있고 효율적인 영어 학습이 가능하도록 하였습니다.

Get Ready Jump 시리즈를 통하여 어린이들이 지속적으로 영어에 대한 흥미와 관심을 가지고 자신의 생각을 정확하고 풍성하게 표현할 수 있게 되기를 바랍니다.

Get Ready Jump

Contents

There Is No Lettuce

DATE /

Pam: Good idea! I can make sandwiches.
Where is the lettuce? There is no lettuce.

Mom: Pam, look on the table.

Pam: Hmm… Mom, where are the eggs? I cannot find them.

Mom: Sorry. There are no eggs.

Pam: May I buy some eggs at the store?

Mom: Sure! Thanks, Pam.

Pam: No problem! Anything else?

Mom: No, that's it.

Role play

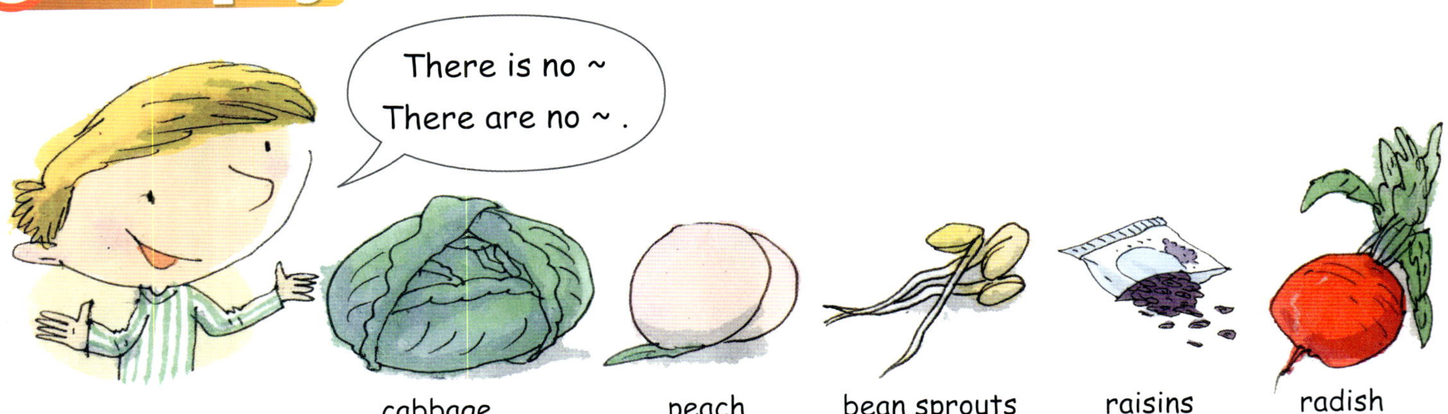

cabbage   peach   bean sprouts   raisins   radish

Reading Zone! 

 **Read the story and answer the questions.**

Let's make a sandwich!
We need lettuce, tomatoes, eggs, and ham.
Let's find them in the fridge.
Oh, my! There is no lettuce.
Oh, dear! There are no eggs, too.
Well, well, it's okay.
I need to go buy some at the store.

 **Answer the questions.**

1. What is she going to make?

    ❶ hotdog   ❷ spaghetti   ❸ sandwich

2. What doesn't she need to make a sandwich?

3. True or False? Circle.

→ There is lettuce in the fridge. | True | False |

Listening Zone!

10 min

1. Listen and repeat. Then trace.

1. lettuce

2. cabbage

3. raisin

4. radish

2. Listen and cross out.

1.

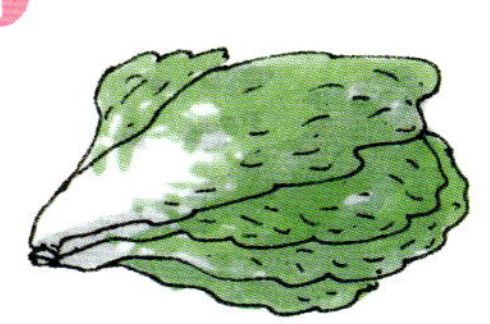
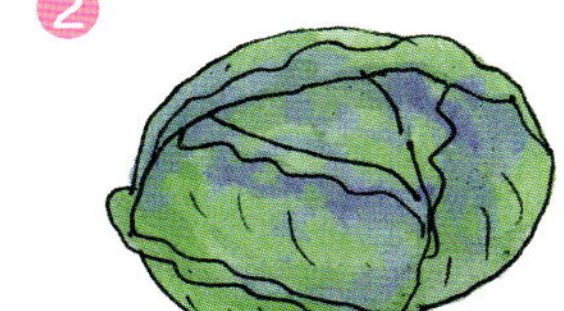

2.

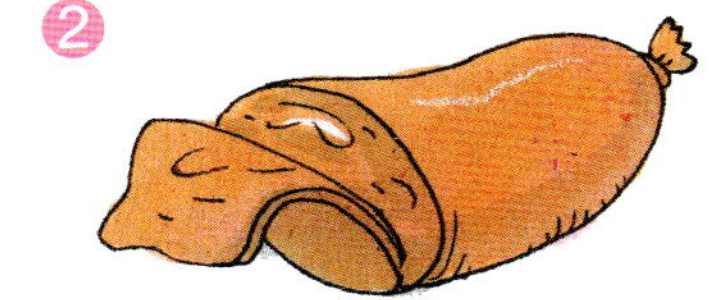
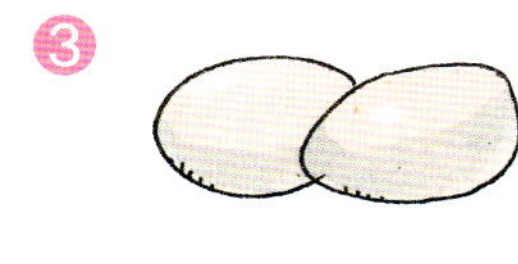

3. Listen and fill in the blanks using the given words.

1. Is there __________ to eat?

2. __________ is no lettuce.

3. __________ are the eggs?

4. There are __________ eggs.

WORD BOX   There   no   Where   anything

Grammar & Writing Zone

15 min

★ Learn and practice.

Positive	Negative
There is ~ .	There is no ~ .
There are ~ .	There are no ~ .

⑥ Change the sentences into negative forms.

1. There are some eggs.

   → There ⬚ ⬚ eggs.

2. There is a radish.

   → There ⬚ ⬚ radish.

✔ Complete the sentences.

There is no lettuce.

1.	There	is	no	lettuce	.
2.	There	is	no		.
3.	There				.
4.					.

Same or Different

Let's **Play**

10 min

Find the differences!

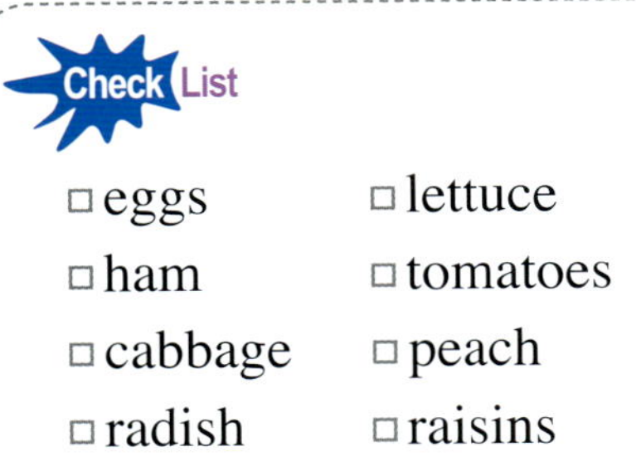

〈Tips!〉 A에는 있는데 B에는 없는 그림을 찾아 There is /are no ~ . 표현을 써서 말해보세요.

 Let's Do It At Home

<table>
<tr><td colspan="2" align="center">check box</td></tr>
<tr><td>parents</td><td></td></tr>
<tr><td>teacher</td><td></td></tr>
</table>

Unit 1

1. Listen and circle.

V / X

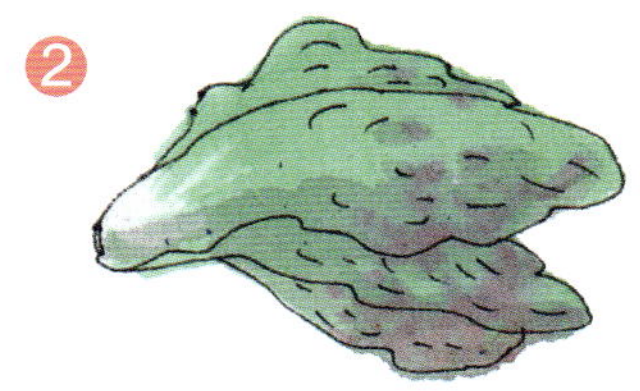

V / X

2. Read and answer.

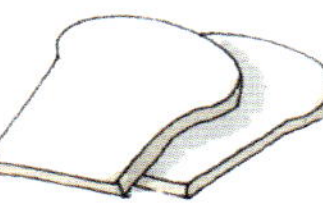

I want to make sandwiches.

I need a tomato, bread, mayonnaise, cheese, and ham.

But there is no cheese in the fridge.

Q: Is there cheese in the fridge? | Yes | No |

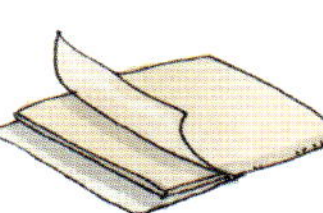

3. Unscramble the sentences.

❶  can / I / sandwiches / make / .

____

❷ are / There / no / more / eggs / .

____

Unit 2

I Am Going To Mike's House

Alice: Why?

Dan: To give this book back.

Alice: Is that Mike's book?

Dan: Yes, I borrowed it for homework.

Alice: Where is his house?

Dan: His house is next to Dora's pizza.

Alice: Mmm, where is Dora's pizza?

Dan: It is next to Kid's toy store.

Alice: Oh, now I see.

Dan: I bet you do. The store is your favorite, isn't it?

☺ Role play

Diego's pet store

Doctor Kim's office

my sister's school

Daddy's auto shop

 **R**eading **Z**one**!**

 **Read the story and answer the questions.**

On the way to Mike's house I met Alice.

She asked where his house was. Mike's house is next to Dora's pizza.

Dora's pizza is my favorite restaurant. But she did not know where it was.

When I said it was next to Kid's toy store, she quickly got it.

Because that toy store is her favorite place.

Answer the questions.

1. Where was Dan going to?
   ❶ Dora's house   ❷ Mike's house   ❸ Alice's house

2. True or False? Circle.
   ❶ Mike's house is next to Dora's pizza.

True	False

   ❷ Kid's toy store is between Dora's pizza and Mike's house.

True	False

 **Listening Zone!** 

1. Listen and repeat. Then trace.

1. **Mike's house**

2. **Dora's pizza**

3. **Doctor Kim's office**

4. **Diego's pet store**

2. Listen and put the stickers on. 

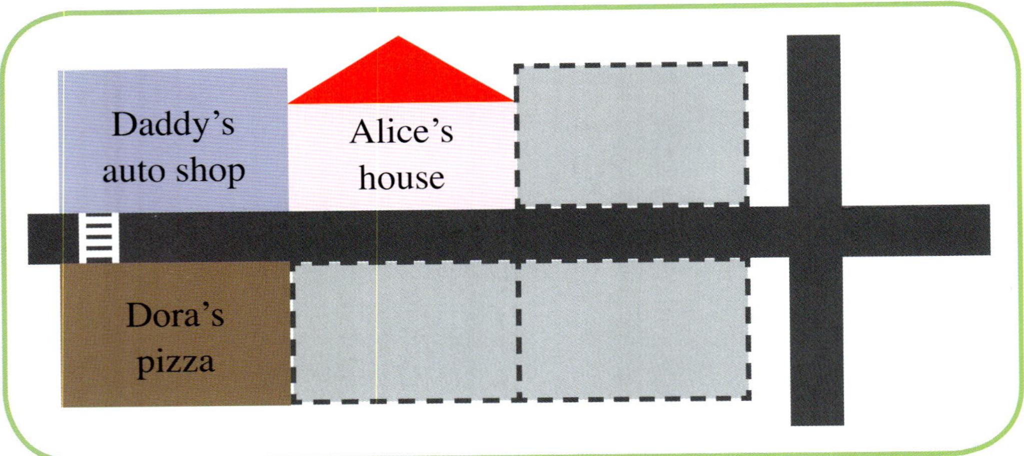

3. Listen and fill in the blanks using the given words.

1. Where are you ⬚ ?

2. I am going to ⬚ house.

3. I ⬚ it for homework.

4. His house is ⬚ to Dora's pizza.

WORD BOX   next   Mike's   borrowed   going

Grammar & Writing Zone
15 min

★ Learn and practice.

Noun	Possessive's
Mike	Mike's house
Dora	Dora's pizza
Diego	Diego's pet store
Doctor Kim	Doctor Kim's office

Correct the sentences.

1. I am going to <u>Dora pizza</u>. → _______________ 

2. Where is <u>Mike house</u>? → _______________ 

3. <u>Diego pet store</u> is next to John's house. → _______________ 

✔ Complete the sentences.

> I am going to Mike's house.

1.	I	am	going	to	Mike's	.
2.	I	am	going			.
3.	I	am				.
4.						.

Where Are You Going?

Spin your clip.

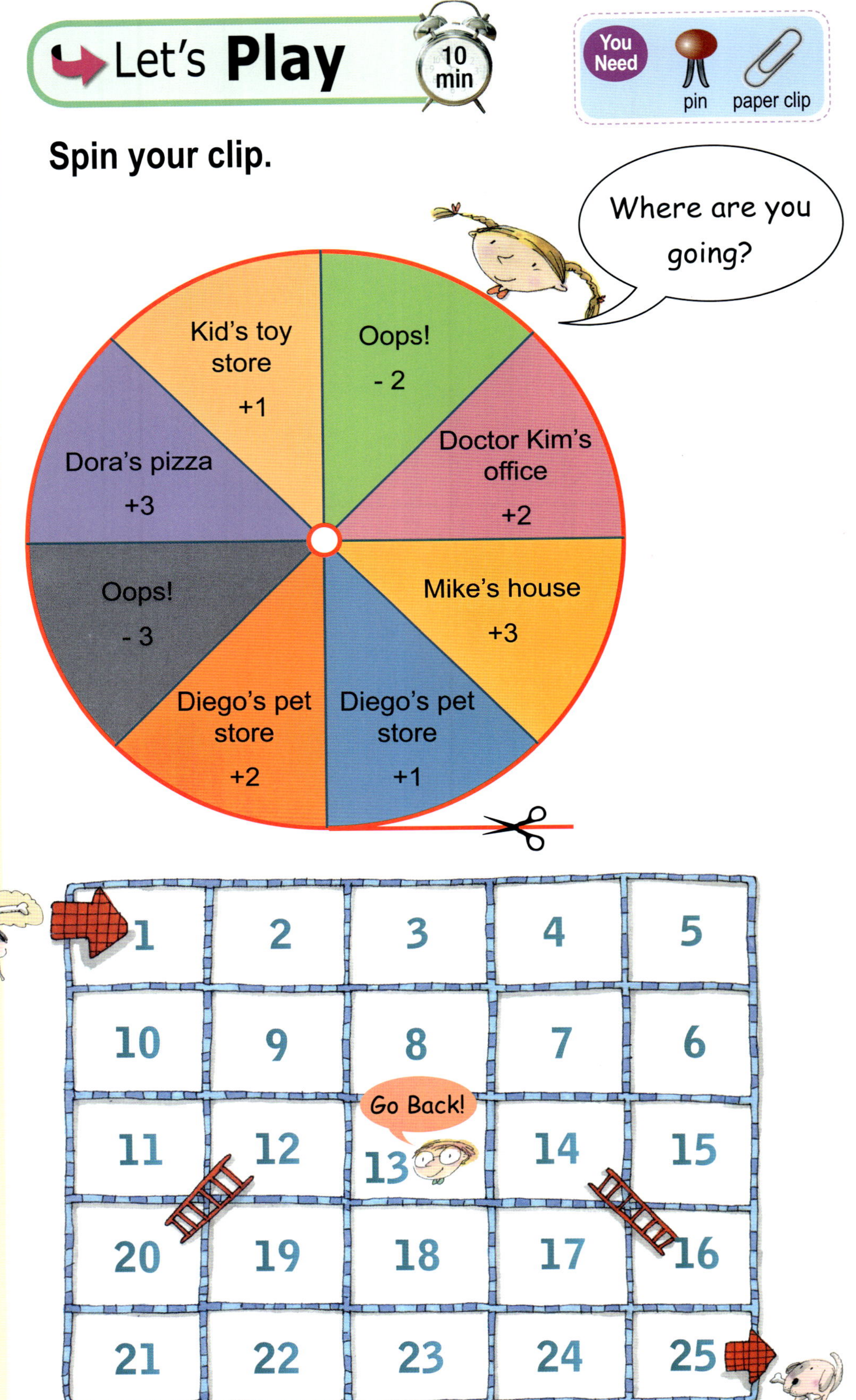

〈Tips!〉 두 팀으로 게임합니다. 가운데 핀을 꽂고 그 핀에 클립을 끼운 후 손가락으로 튕겨서 나온 지점에서 Where are you going? I am going ~이라는 대화를 연습하면서 나온 숫자만큼 앞으로 가거나 뒤로 갑니다. 먼저 25를 다 빠져나오는 팀이 이깁니다.
－'Go Back'에서는 이전의 번호로 돌아갑니다.

 Let's Do It At Home

check box	
parents	
teacher	

1. Listen and circle.

①

ⓐ

ⓑ

②

ⓐ

ⓑ

2. Read and circle.

A: Mary, where are you going?
B: I am going to my sister's school.
A: Where is it?
B: It is next to Kid's toy store.

| Diego's pet store | school ❶ | | Dara's pizza | school ❷ |
| school ❸ | Mike's house | | Kid's toy store | school ❹ |

3. Unscramble the sentences.

❶ book / that / Is / Mike's / ?

____

❷ His house / pizza / Dora's / is / next to / .

His house __________________________________

Unit 3 — It Is Mine

Scott: Whose bike is this?

Tina: It's mine.

Scott: It is so nice!

Tina: Yes! But John's is nicer than mine.

Scott: Does he have a bike, too?

Tina: Yes, his is brand-new.

Scott: Wow, I'm jealous of you guys.

Tina: Why, Scott?
　　　Don't you have a bike?

Scott: Not really. Mine is
　　　just for young kids.

Tina: Oh, sorry. You can
　　　use mine if you want.

Scott: Thanks!

😊 Role play

WORD BOX	
mine	his
yours	hers
ours	theirs

scooter

toy car

skateboard

 **R**eading **Z**one**!**

 **Read the story and answer the questions.**

> Do you have a bike?
> Actually, I have one but
> mine is just for young kids.
> Tina has a nice bike.
> Hers is a shiny green one.
> John also has a bike.
> It is brand-new and electric!
> I wish I had a nice bike, too.

✿ Answer the questions.

1. Does Scott have a bike?　　　Yes ◯　　No ◯

2. What color is Tina's bike?

❶ 　❷ 　❸ 　❹ 

3. Choose the correct word and fill in the blank.

   John's bike is an electric one.

   = _______________ is an electric one.

1. Listen and repeat. Then trace.

1. **mine**

2. **hers**

3. **his**

4. **yours**

2. Listen and match.

his

hers

mine

3. Listen and fill in the blanks using the given words.

1. ____________ bike is this?

2. It is ____________ .

3. John's is ____________ than mine.

4. ____________ is brand-new.

WORD BOX   nicer   His   mine   Whose

Grammar & Writing Zone  10 min

⭐ Learn and practice.

Possessive Pronoun		

my		→	mine
your	+ noun	→	yours
his		→	his
her		→	hers

🌀 Read and fill in the blanks.

1. My bike is green. = ________________ is green.

2. Her scooter is nice. = ________________ is nice.

3. His car is brand new. = ________________ is brand-new.

WORD BOX Hers His Mine

✔ Complete the sentences.

Whose bike is this?

1.	Whose	bike	is	this	?
2.	Whose	bike	is		?
3.	Whose				?
4.					?

You Need

CD player

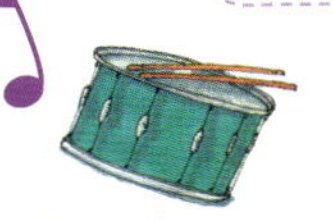

 Let's chant together.

Whose bike is this?
Whose bike is this?
It's mine. It's my bike.
Where is my bike?
Where is mine?
Yours is there. Your bike is there.
Whose scooter is this?
Whose scooter is this?
It's hers. It's her scooter.
Where is his scooter?
Where is his?
His is here.
His scooter is here.
Oh! I see. Thank you.

Unscramble the words.

1. My bike = imen →

2. Your bike = rsoyu →

3. Her scooter = shre →

4. His scooter = sih →

〈Tips!〉 즐겁게 챈트를 따라해보고 아래의 단어활동 문제를 풀어보세요.

Let's Do It At Home

	check box
parents	
teacher	

1. Listen and circle.

① 

ⓐ　　　ⓑ

② 

ⓐ　　　ⓑ

2. Read and match.

①  His bike is nice. •

②  Her scooter is red. •

③ My ball is big. •

ⓐ • Hers is red.

ⓑ • Mine is big.

ⓒ • His is nice.

3. Unscramble the sentences.

① mine / is / It / .

____

② brand-new / is / His / .

____

Is He Tall?

DATE   /

1

Max: Scott, what are you doing here?
Scott: I am looking for my friend.
Max: Is he a member of the band?
Scott: Yes, he is. I promised to take a
        picture of him.

2

Max: What does he look like? Is he tall?
Scott: No, he isn't.
Max: Is he thin?
Scott: No, he is not thin. He is a little
        chubby.

3

Max: Is his hair blond?
Scott: No, it isn't. He has black hair.
Max: Look there! Is that your friend?
Scott: Yes! Max. Thanks.

Role play

short

fat

stout

slim

skinny

 **R**eading **Z**one!

 **Read the story and answer the questions.**

Scott was looking for his friend in the school marching band at the parade. Max was helping him.

"Is he tall? Or is he thin?" asked Max.

"No, he is not tall and he is not thin," answered Scott.

"Is your friend that boy?" asked Max, pointing to a short and chubby boy.

"Yes! Thanks, Max," said Scott.

 **Answer the questions.**

1. Where were Scott and Max?

   ❶ at a circus   ❷ at a parade   ❸ at a zoo   ❹ at a mall

2. Who was Scott looking for?

   ❶ Friend   ❷ Max   ❸ Teacher   ❹ Brother

3. Circle two words.

   → Scott's friend is [＿＿＿＿] and [＿＿＿＿] .

   ❶ short   ❷ tall   ❸ thin   ❹ chubby

1. Listen and repeat. Then trace.

1. chubby
2. stout
3. slim
4. skinny

2. Listen and circle.

1. 

V / X

2. 

V / X

3. Listen and fill in the blanks using the given words.

1. I am looking for my [   ] .

2. [   ] he a member of the band?

3. Is he [   ] ?

4. Is his hair [   ] ?

WORD BOX   Is   blond   thin   friend

Grammar & Writing Zone

10 min

⭐ Learn and practice.

Adjective	Question				
thin	Am	I		thin	
tall	Is	he / she	+	tall	?
stout	Are	you / we / they		stout	

🌀 Unscramble the sentences.

1. thin / I / Am / ?　　➡　________________________

2. he / Is / tall / ?　　➡　________________________

3. stout / Are / you / ?　　➡　________________________

✔ Complete the sentences.

> Is he tall ?

1.	Is	he	tall	?
2.	Is	he		?
3.	Is			?
4.				?

Adjective Card Game

Let's **Play** 10 min

What does he look like?

Is he thin?

Is he tall?

Is he chubby?

Is he short?

Is he fat?

Is he skinny?

〈Tips!〉 스무고개 게임과 비슷합니다. 가위로 카드를 오려서 해도 되고 오리지 않아도 됩니다. 두 팀으로 나누어서 게임합니다. 가위로 오리지 않을 경우 한 팀에서 괴물 중 하나를 마음 속에 정합니다. 상대편이 돌아가며 옆에 있는 질문들을 이용해서 어떤 괴물인지 알아맞히는 게임있니다. 질문해서 다섯 번 안에 맞추면 점수를 얻고 다섯 번 안에 못맞추면 기회를 잃고 상대편이 괴물을 고르게 됩니다. 가위로 오릴 경우 괴물을 고른 편은 고른 괴물을 숨겨두고 상대편이 다섯 번 질문을 끝내면 보여줍니다.

Let's Do It At Home

1. Listen and circle.

①    ②    ③ 

2. Read and circle.

① A: Is he chubby?
B: No, he isn't. He is thin.

ⓐ   ⓑ

② A: Is she skinny?
B: Yes, she is. She is skinny.

ⓐ   ⓑ

3. Unscramble the sentences.

① thin / he / Is / ?

____

② is / He / chubby / a little / .

____

Unit 5 — Let's Go To The Dinosaur Museum!

DATE   /

18

❶

❷

❸

❹

❺

❻

Role play

buy a ticket

ask to the guide

tour the museum

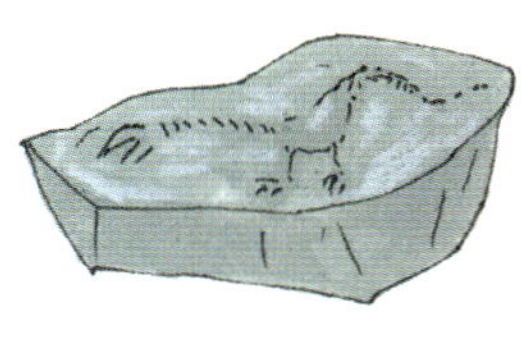

go see the fossils

 Reading Zone!

10 min

Read the story and answer the questions.

On the way home Pam and Tina were talking about their dinosaur homework.

"Let's go to the dinosaur museum!" said Tina.

At the museum, they saw a big dinosaur fossil.

"Let's take a picture!" said Pam. While they were going back home, they talked excitedly.

"It was so fun. Let's come back again!"

 Answer the questions.

1. What was the homework about?
   ❶ museums ❷ pictures ❸ dinosaurs ❹ models

2. Draw lines between ❶, ❷, and ❸ in order to complete the sentences from the story above.

❶ Let's	•	•	take	•	•	the museum!
❷ Let's	•	•	go to	•	•	again!
❸ Let's	•	•	come back	•	•	a picture!

1. Listen and repeat. Then trace.

1. **museum**

2. **dinosaur**

3. **guide**

4. **fossils**

2. Listen and number in order.

3. Listen and fill in the blanks using the given words.

1. __________ go to the museum.

2. That's a good __________ .

3. Look at the __________ .

4. Let's take a __________ .

WORD BOX   dinosaur   idea   picture   Let's

Grammar & Writing Zone 

★ Learn and practice.

Verb	Suggestion - Let's
go	Let's go to the museum!
take	Let's take a picture!
use	Let's use the map!
buy	Let's buy some gifts!

Circle the correct suggestion sentence.

1.
❶ We must use the map.
❷ Let's use the map!

2.
❶ I buy some flowers.
❷ Let's buy some flowers.

✔ Complete the sentences.

Let's go to the dinosaur museum!

1. Let's | go | to | the | dinosaur | | !
2. Let's | go | to | | | | !
3. Let's | | | | | | !
4. | | | | | | !

Pictures In The Picture

Let's Play 10 min

You Need pencil

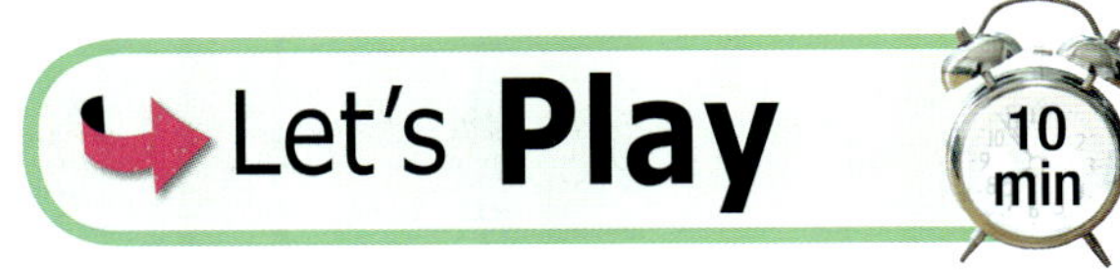

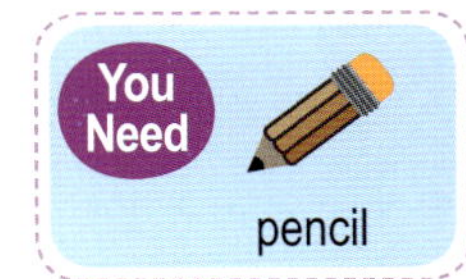

Find the girls and boys!

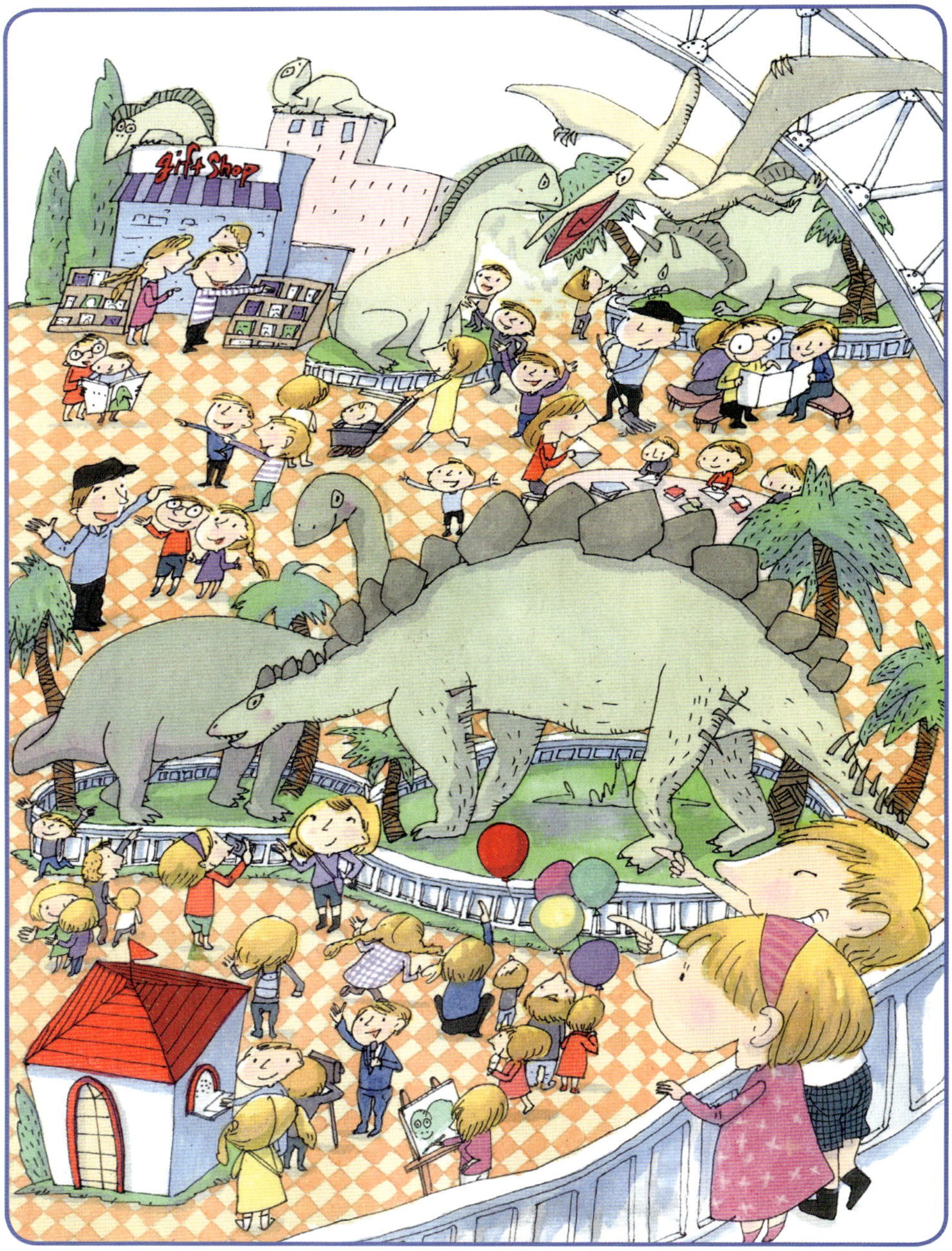

1. A boy and a girl: "Let's buy a ticket!"
2. Two girls: "Let's take a picture!"
3. Two boys: "Let's use the map!"
4. A boy and a girl: "Let's ask the guide!"
5. A boy and a girl: "Let's buy some gifts!"

〈Tips!〉 문장을 읽고 해당하는 그림을 찾아 동그라미 하세요.

1. Listen and circle.

1

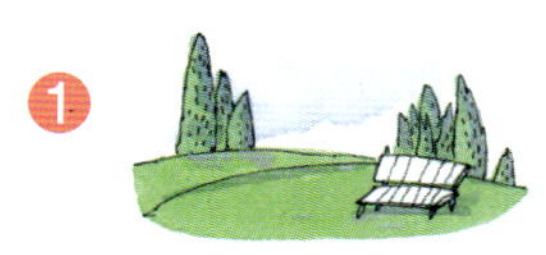
ⓐ

ⓑ

ⓒ

2

ⓐ

ⓑ

ⓒ

2. Read and match.

1 Let's go to the museum! •

2 Let's take a picture! •

3 Let's use the map! •

• ⓐ 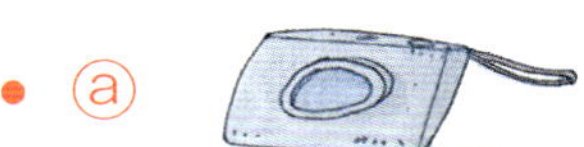

• ⓑ 

• ⓒ 

3. Unscramble the sentences.

1 picture / take / Let's / a / !

____

2 use / Let's / map / the / !

____

Unit 6 — You Should Stop Eating Too Much Candy

22

Doctor: What's the matter?

Bob: My teeth hurt.

Doctor: Say ahh.

Bob: Ahh-.

Doctor: You have cavities.
Do you eat many sweets?

Bob: Yes, I love candy and I eat sweets everyday.

Doctor: You should stop eating too much candy.

Bob: Oh, no!

Doctor: You should brush your teeth often, too.

Bob: Oh, dear!

Role play

**R**eading **Zone!**

 **Read the story and answer the questions.**

Last night I woke up with a toothache.

It hurt so much that I went to see a dentist.

The dentist said I had cavities.

He said I should stop eating too much candy and should brush my teeth more often.

Mom hid the candy jars and bought three toothbrushes.

Oh, dear me!

 **Answer the questions.**

1. What's wrong with Bob? Circle.

   He had a …   ❶    ❷    ❸ 

2. What should Bob do? Fill in the blanks.

   ❶ He should [   ] eating too much candy. 

   ❷ He should [   ] his teeth often. 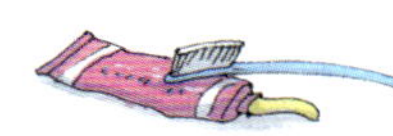

   exercise   stop   drink   brush

Listening Zone!

1. Listen and repeat. Then trace.

1. brush your teeth

2. stop eating sweets

3. eat vegetable

4. take a shower

2. Listen and number in order.

3. Listen and fill in the blanks using the given words.

1. What's the [   ]?

2. You have [   ].

3. You [   ] stop eating sweets.

4. You should [   ] your teeth often.

WORD BOX   cavities   should   matter   brush

Grammar & Writing Zone

★ Learn and practice.

Verb	Advice - should		
stop			stop
brush	should	+	brush
exercise			exercise

Circle the proper advice.

1. 
   ❶ You should take a shower.
   ❷ You should exercise often.

2. ❶ You should brush your teeth often.
   ❷ You should wash your hands.

✔ Complete the sentences.

You should brush your teeth often.

1. | You | should | brush | your | teeth | | . |

2. | You | should | brush | your | | | . |

3. | You | should | | | | | . |

4. | | | | | | | . |

Be a doctor and give your advice card to your patients.

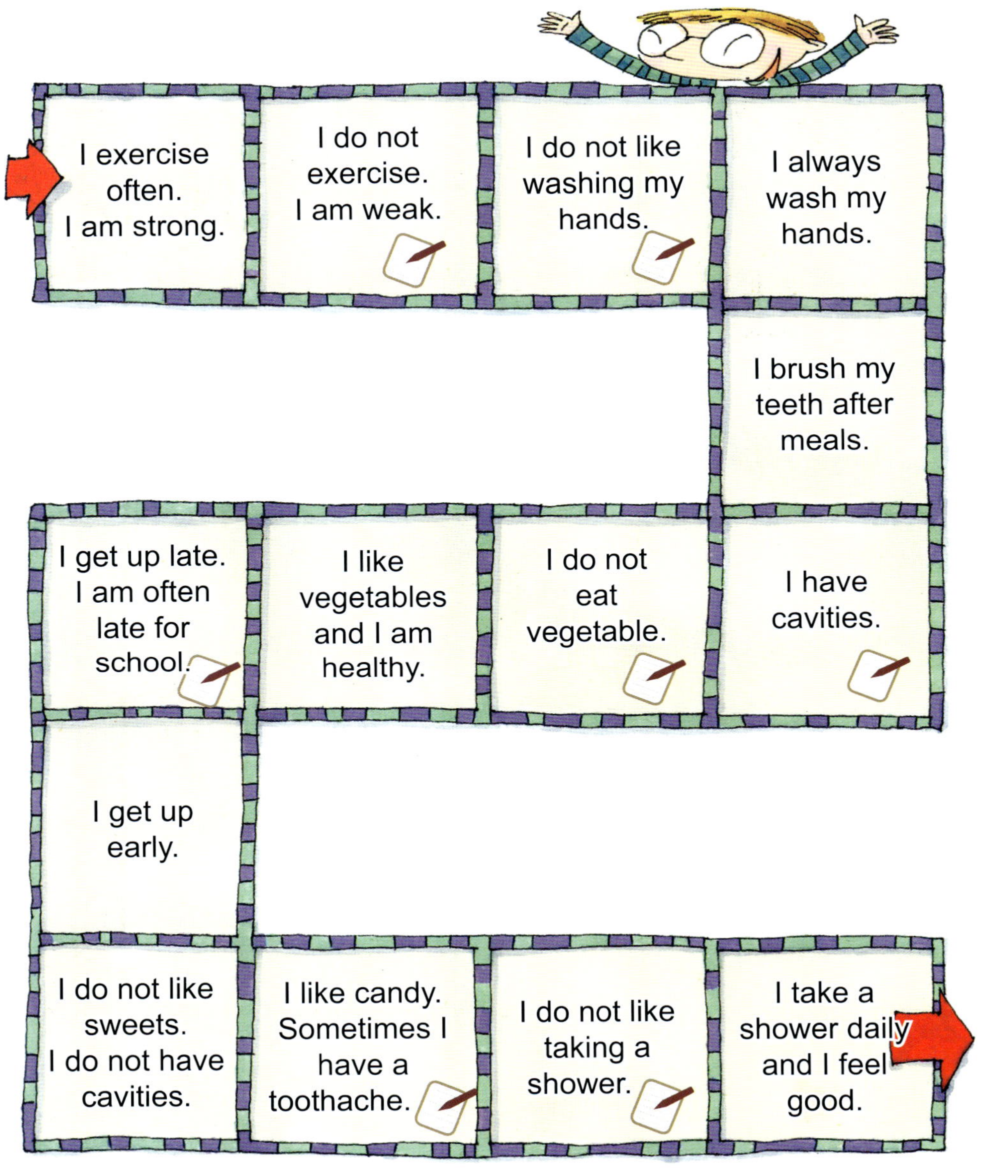

You should exercise often.

You should wash your hands.

You should brush your teeth often.

You should eat vegetable.

You should get up early.

You should stop eating too much candy.

You should take a shower.

〈Tips!〉두 팀으로 게임합니다. 동전을 던져서 앞면이 나오면 한 칸, 뒷면이 나오면 두 칸 갑니다. '종이위에 연필'그림이 있는 칸에 오면 상대방이 그 내용에 알맞은 충고카드를 읽어주고 충고 카드를 줍니다. 충고카드를 많이 가진 쪽이 집니다.

1. Listen and circle.

2. Read and fill in the blanks.

1. My hands are dirty.

➜ You should __________ your hands.

2. I got up late and I was late for school.

➜ You should __________ up early.

WORD BOX   stop   wash   eat   get

3. Unscramble and make sentences.

❶ exercise / often / should / You / .

____

❷ should / hands / You / your / wash / .

____

Unit 7 — I Am As Brave As Him

DATE   /

26

1

2

3

4

5

6

Role play

clever   beautiful   rich   thin   fast

Read the story and answer the questions.

At the circus, a brave man was training a lion. I thought I was as brave as him. But I screamed when I saw a spider. I tried to lift a big rock. But I couldn't. I fell on my bottom. Oh-oh! Not again! However, a kind tall man lifted me up and said I could be as tall as him! Yahoo!

Answer the questions.

1. Circle the correct picture according to the story above.

2. Fill in the blanks using the given words.

Max wanted to be ________________ him.

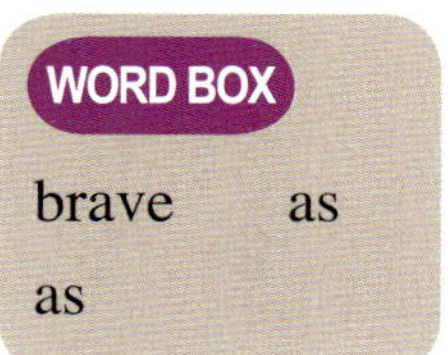

1. Listen and repeat. Then trace.

1. **as brave as**
2. **as strong as**
3. **as tall as**
4. **as clever as**

2. Listen and circle.

1. 

2.  

3. Listen and fill in the blanks using the given words.

1. He is so [______].

2. I am as brave [______] him.

3. I am as [______] as him.

4. Max, [______] out!

WORD BOX   as   strong   brave   watch

Grammar & Writing Zone

★ Learn and practice.

Adjective	Comparison Of Adjective (No Difference)
brave	brave
strong	as + strong + as
tall	tall

🌀 Fill in the blanks.

1. I am ☐ ☐ ☐ him.

2. I am ☐ ☐ ☐ her.

✔ Complete the sentences.

> I am as brave as him.

1. I am as brave as ________ .

2. I am as brave ________ ________ .

3. I am ________ ________ ________ .

4. ________ .

Sentence Tetris

I am as brave as you.

I am as clever as you.

I am as rich as you.

I am as fast as you.

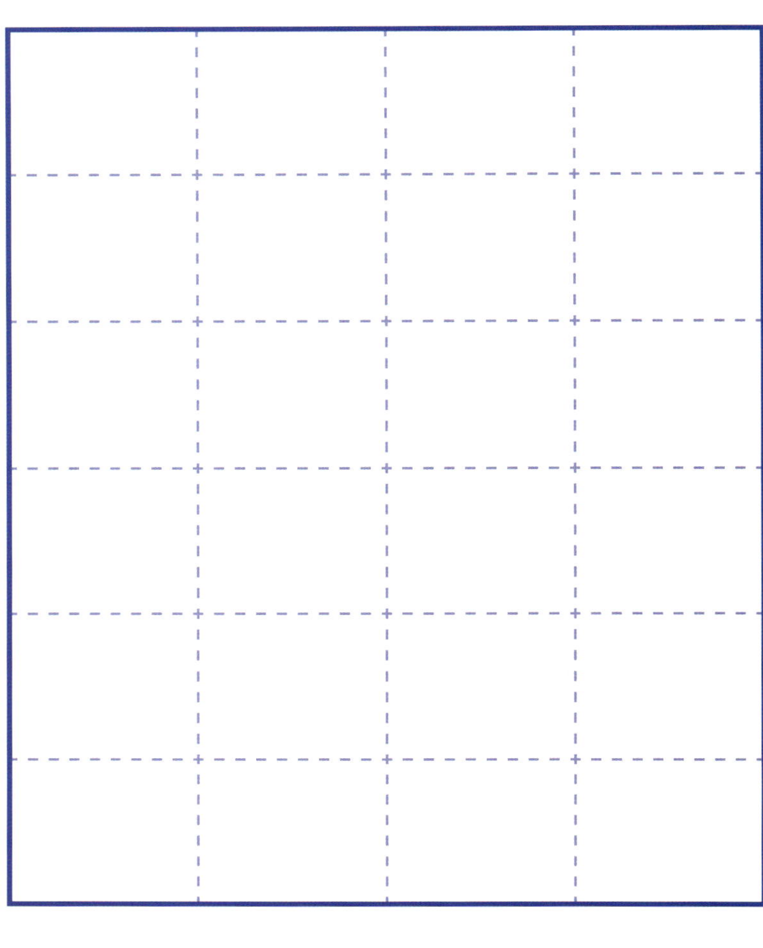

I am as tall as you.

I am as strong as you.

〈Tips!〉 작은 블럭들을 직사각형 큰 판에 맞추어 직사각형 모양을 만듭니다. 다 맞춘후 한 문장씩 읽습니다.

Let's Do It At Home

1. Listen and number in order.

2. Read and match.

❶ The boy is as tall as Max. •

❷ The girl is as thin as the boy. •

❸ The boy is as fast as the girl. •

• ⓐ 

• ⓑ 

• ⓒ 

3. Unscramble the sentences.

❶ brave / so / is / He / .

____

❷ am / as / him / I / as / strong / .

____

Unit 8 — Do You Want A Pet Or A Toy?

DATE   /

30

Dad: Bob, your birthday is coming. What do you want for a present?
Bob: Wow! I am thinking.
Dad: Do you want a pet or a toy?
Bob: A pet? That's good! I want a pet.
Dad: What do you want? Do you want a dog or a cat?
Bob: Well… I want neither.
Dad: How about a bird or a fish?
Bob: That's it. I want a bird.
Dad: Do you want a parrot or a parakeet?
Bob: Parrot! Wow! Do you really mean it?
Dad: Sure! I mean it!
Bob: Thank you, dad! I love you!

turtle

goldfish

hamster

rabbit

 **Reading Zone!** (15 min)

Read the story and answer the questions.

Today, dad bought a parrot!

I named him Pepe.

Pepe needed a lot to live with me.

A cage, some food, a feeder, a stand and so on.

It was not easy to prepare all of these things.

Sometimes I ask Pepe what it wants to eat:

"Do you want peanuts or veggie?"

Then Pepe just repeats what I say:

"Peanuts or veggie. Peanuts or veggie."

 **Answer the questions.**

1. What did dad buy for Bob?

   ❶ 　　　❷ 　　　❸ 

2. What is the parrot's name?

   ❶ Peanut　　　❷ Pepe　　　❸ Veggie　　　❹ Parrot

3. True or False? Circle.

   → Bob bought peanuts for Pepe.　　　　| True | False |

Listening Zone!

1. Listen and repeat. Then trace.

1. pet

2. parrot

3. parakeet

4. hamster

2. Listen and circle.

1.

Anna

ⓐ　　ⓑ

2.

David

ⓐ　　ⓑ

3. Listen and fill in the blanks using the given words.

1. What do you want for a (______)?

2. I want (______).

3. How about a bird or a (______)?

4. Do you want a parrot or a (______)?

WORD BOX　　neither　　fish　　present　　parakeet

Grammar & Writing Zone  10 min

 **Learn and practice.**

Choice Question
Do you want a pet or a toy?
Do you want a dog or a cat?
Do you want a parrot or a parakeet?

Make choice questions using the given words.

1. a turtle / a rabbit

→ Do you want ☐ ☐ ☐ ?

2. a hamster / a goldfish

→ Do you want ☐ ☐ ☐ ?

Complete the sentences.

Do you want a pet or a toy?

1.	Do	you	want	a	pet	or	a		?
2.	Do	you	want	a	pet	or			?
3.	Do	you	want						?
4.									?

Do you want a dog or a cat?

A dog

A cat

A parrot

A parakeet

A goldfish

A turtle

A rabbit

A hamster

A toy

〈Tips!〉 전체 카드 중 두 장을 골라 상대방에게 보여주며 묻습니다. 예를 들어 a dog와 a cat카드를 보여주며 Do you want a dog or a cat?이라고 물어봅니다. 그리고 상대방이 볼 수 없게 손을 뒤로 돌리거나 책상 아래 넣어서 두 카드 중 하나만을 골라 손에 들고 있습니다. 그러면 상대방이 I want ~ . 이라며 대답합니다. 그 대답이 가지고 있는 카드와 일치하면 점수를 얻습니다.

Let's Do It At Home 

check box
parents	
teacher	

1. Listen and match.

 ①  ② ③ 

ⓐ  ⓑ  ⓒ 

2. Read and circle.

A: Sara, what do you want for a present?

Do you want a hamster or a rabbit?

B: I do not like hamsters. I want a rabbit.

Q: What does Sara want?

①  ②  ③ 

3. Unscramble the sentences.

❶ pet / want / I / a / .

____

❷ you / Do / a / want / or / dog / cat / a / ?

____

Who Will Help Me Bake A Cake?

DATE   /

1

2

3

4

5

6

Role play

pour the water

sift the flour

frost the cake

cool the cookies

Reading Zone!

Read the story and answer the questions.

I baked a cake today.
① I asked Bob, Max and Pam to help me make the cake.
But they all said, "No."
When I was done, I asked them, "Who will help me eat the cake?"
This time everybody said, "Me, me!"
You know what? They did not help me, so I ate it up by myself. Yummy!

Answer the questions.

1. What did she do today? Circle.

Bake a cake

Make cookies

Cook a hotdog

2. What did she ask her friends? Fill in the blanks using the sentence ①.
Sue: "Who will ____________ me ____________ a cake?

3. Who ate the cake?
❶ All   ❷ Bob and Sue   ❸ Sue alone   ❹ Max

Listening Zone!  

1. Listen and repeat. Then trace.

1. grease
2. mash
3. beat
4. pour

2. Listen and draw a line.

1.    pour the water

2.    grease the pan

3.    mash the bananas

3. Listen and fill in the blanks using the given words.

1. __________ will help me bake a cake?

2. __________ me. I am busy.

3. Who will help me __________ the bananas?

4. I will eat it up by __________ .

WORD BOX   Not   Who   myself   mash

Grammar & Writing Zone

15 min

Learn and practice.

Verb	WH Question - WHO
bake	bake
make	make
beat	Who will help me ~ beat ~ ?
mash	mash

Fill in the blanks.

1. ____________ will help me bake a cake?

2. Who ____________ help me make some cookies?

3. Who will ____________ me mash the bananas?

WORD BOX   will   Who   help

Complete the sentences.

Who will help me bake a cake?

1. | Who | will | help | me | bake | a | | ? |

2. | Who | will | help | me | | | | ? |

3. | Who | will | | | | | ? |

4. | | | | | | | ? |

Make Cookies!

Put the stickers for the missing things!

Who will help me make the cake?

Who will help me bake some cookies?

Who will help me mash the bananas?

Who will help me grease the pan?

Who will help me beat the cake mix and bananas?

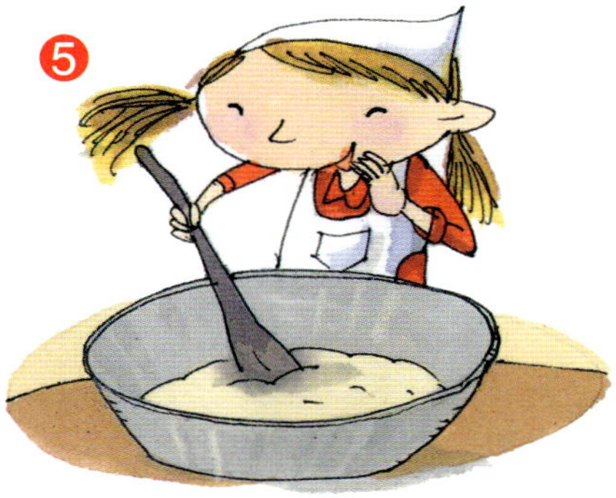

〈Tips!〉 그림을 보고 해당하는 말풍선 스티커를 찾아 붙여보세요.

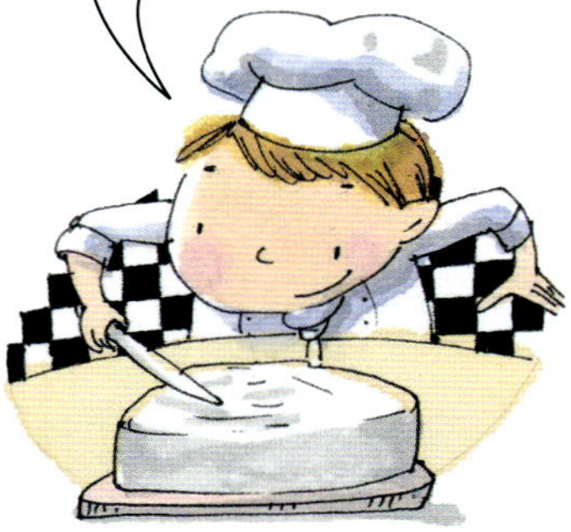

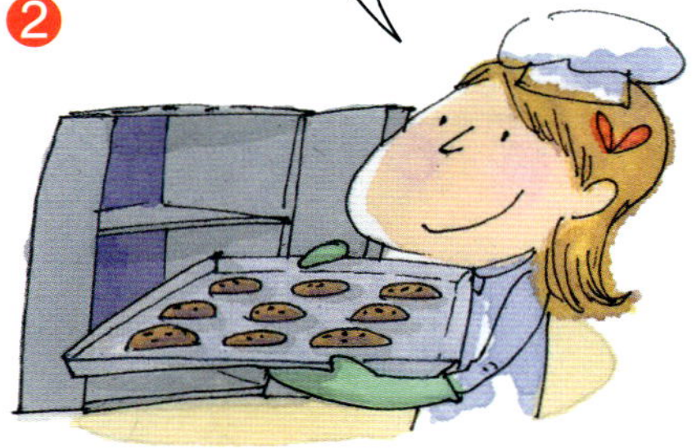

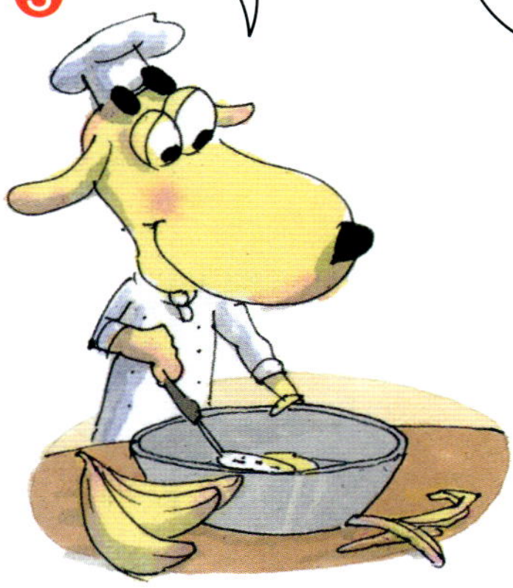

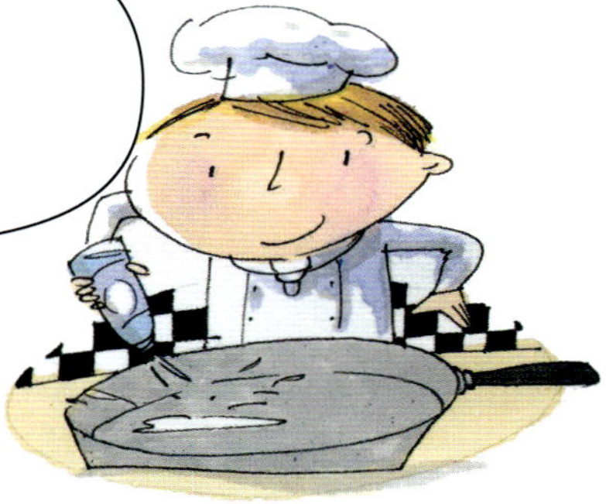

Let's Do It At Home

check box

parents	
teacher	

1. Listen and circle.

1

ⓐ

ⓑ

2

ⓐ

ⓑ

2. Circle the correct word.

1 Who will help me ______ the pan?

grease
beat

2 Who will help me ______ a cake?

bake
pour

3. Unscramble the sentences.

1 my / to / I / do / have / homework / .

____

2 the cake / help / make / You / me / did not / .

____

What Does It Say?

DATE /

38

Role play

the left

the east

the south

the north

Read the story and answer the questions.

I found a treasure map.
It says…

Sail through the wild sea.
Climb up the high mountains.

At last I found some treasure!
Suddenly, I heard pirates coming
after me.
I tried to run away but my legs did
not move. Oh, no!
I tried hard and I woke up.

Answer the questions.

1. What does the treasure map say? Fill in the blanks.

   ❶ [   ] through the wild sea.

   ❷ [   ] up the high mountains.

2. Write numbers in order according to the story.

1. Listen and repeat. Then trace.

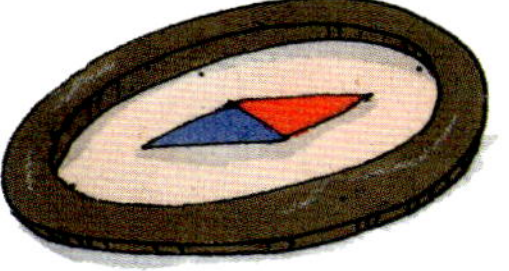

1. the east

2. the west

3. the south

4. the north

2. Listen and circle.

1. ❶ 

❷ 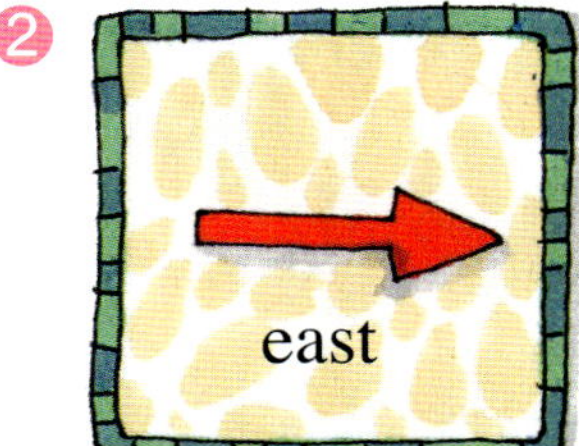

❸ 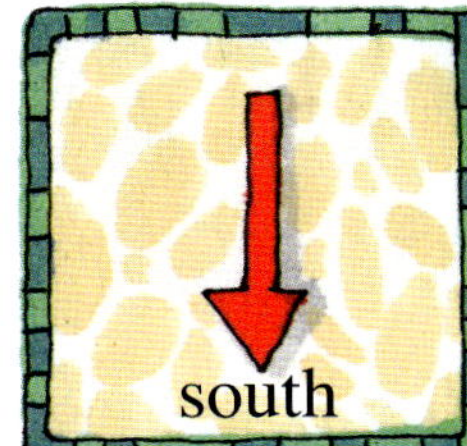

2. ❶ 

❷ 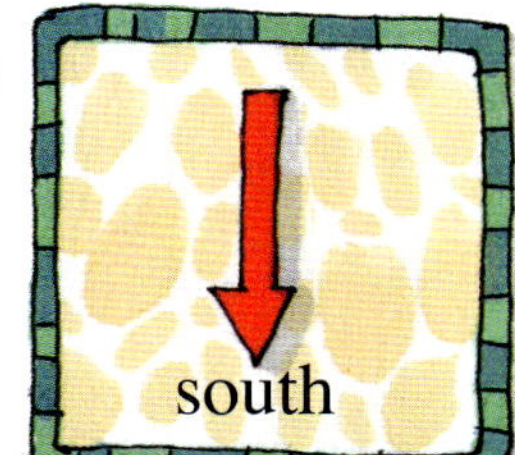

❸ 

3. Listen and fill in the blanks using the given words.

1. [   ] does it say?

2. It [   ], "Ten steps to the right."

3. It says, "Five [   ] to the west."

4. It says, "[   ] there."

WORD BOX   says   steps   What   Dig

Grammar & Writing Zone

⭐ **Learn and practice.**

WH Question - WHAT

		it				
What does	+	she	+	verb	~	?
		he				

🌀 **Unscramble and write.**

1. does / What / say / it / ?   → _______________________

2. she / does / What / say / ?   → _______________________

3. say / What / he / does / ?   → _______________________

✔ **Complete the sentences.**

It says, "Five steps to the west."

1.	It	says,	"Five	steps	to			."
2.	It	says,	"Five					."
3.	It	says,						."
4.								."

Treasure Hunt

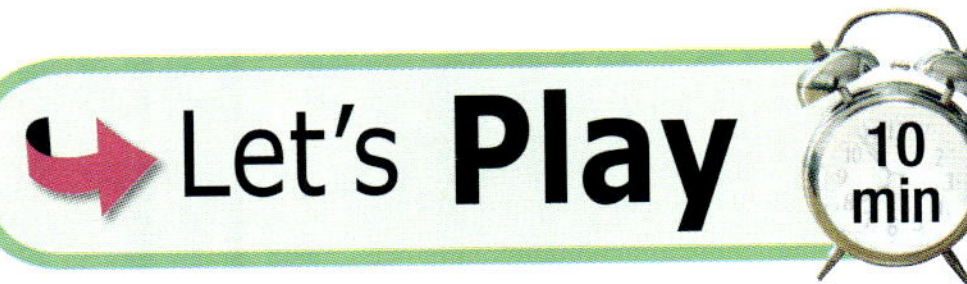

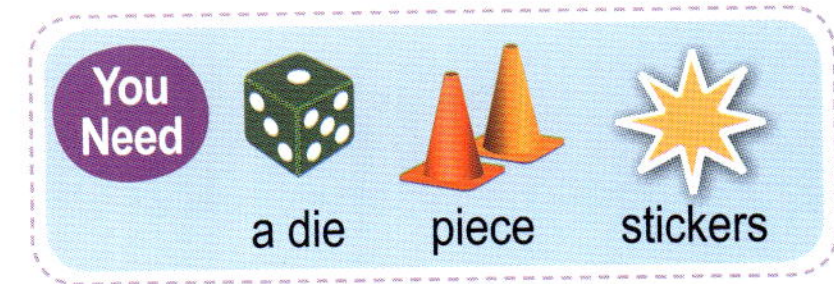

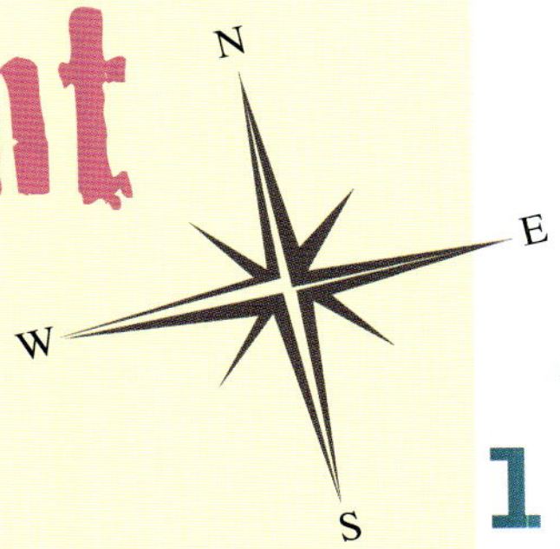

Let's Play 10 min

You Need: a die, piece, stickers

At your turn, move your marker according to the direction.

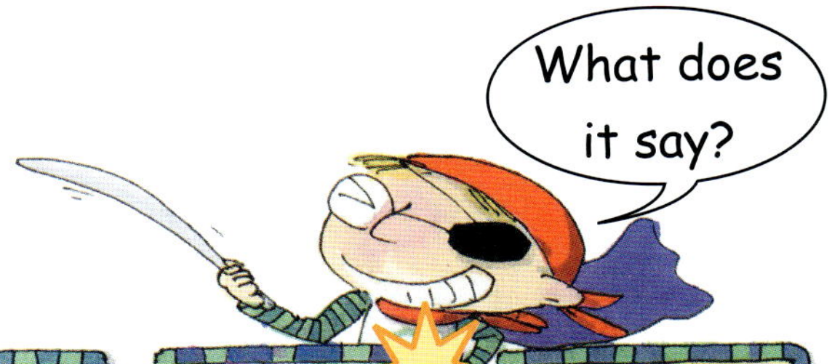

1	Two steps to the east.	Two steps to the south.	One step to the east.	Miss your turn.
2	One step to the north.	Two steps to the east.	Miss your turn	Three steps to the west.
3	One step to the east.	Miss your turn	Two steps to the north.	One step to the north.
4	Three steps to the east	Two steps to the north.	Two steps to the west.	One step to the south.
5, 6	Two steps to the east.	One step to the east.	Miss your turn	Two steps to the west.

My Treasure Box

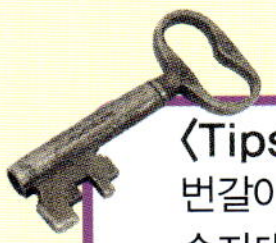

〈Tips!〉 두 팀으로 나눕니다. 스티커에 있는 보물 10개를 이용합니다. 처음에 주사위를 던져서 나온 숫자에서 출발합니다. 한번에 번갈아가며 주어진 지시사항대로 한번씩만 움직입니다. "Miss your turn."에서는 한번 기회를 잃고 다음 기회에 주사위를 던져서 나온 숫자대로 움직입니다. 각자 편의 말들이 보물이 그려진 지점에 놓이면 그 팀이 보물스티커를 하나 가져갑니다. 보물 10개가 다 없어질때까지 게임을 하고, 보물을 더 많이 가진 팀이 승리합니다.

Let's Do It At Home

1. Listen and write.

1 One step to the [ ].

2 Two steps to the [ ].

3 Three steps to the [ ].

2. What does it say? Read and circle.

It says …

One step to the east at the cave,
Then two steps to the north,
Then one step to the west.

→ Answer [ ]

3. Unscramble the sentences.

1   does / What / say / it / ?

____

2   to / steps / ten / right / the / .

It says, ___________________________

They Are Helping People

DATE   /

Mike: What is that sound?

Joey: Let's go and find out.

Mike: Look! It's a fire!

Joey: Yes! There are firefighters, too.

Mike: What are they doing?

Joey: They are pulling out the hose.

Mike: Look at the long ladder!

Joey: They are climbing up the ladder!

Mike: Look! The fire is dying.

Joey: Yes! There is so much smoke.

Mike: See. The firefighters are helping people.

Joey: Yeah, they are real heroes!

Role play

connecting the hose to the hydrant

spraying water

saving people

Reading **Z**one**!**

Read the story and answer the questions.

Today, there was a fire near my house.

When I went out, firefighters were pulling out the hose.

They started spraying water on the fire.

Soon, the fire was out.

But the firefighters were still working.

They were helping people.

What brave people they are!

They were real heroes!

 **Answer the questions.**

1. True or False? Circle.

❶ It was Mike's house on fire.

True	False

❷ The fire was out soon.

True	False

2. Circle the things that the firefighters did in the story.

❶  ❷  ❸  ❹ 

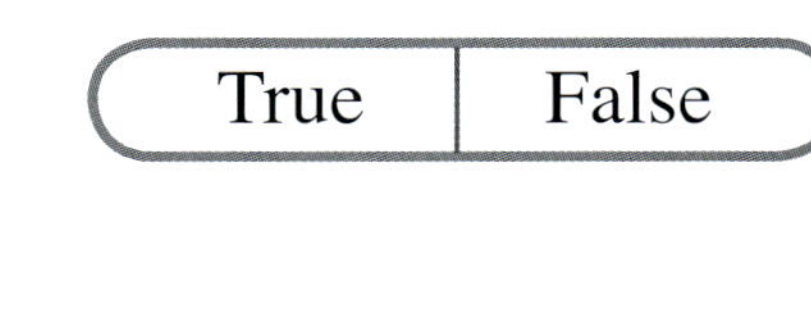

1. Listen and repeat. Then trace.

1. **pulling out the hose**
2. **climbing the ladder**
3. **helping people**
4. **spraying water**

2. Listen and number.

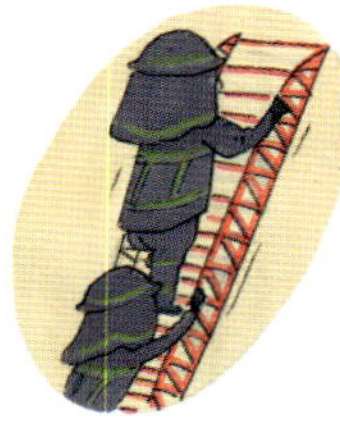 

3. Listen and fill in the blanks using the given words.

1. What is that (   ) ?

2. (   ) is a fire!

3. What are they (   ) ?

4. They are real (   ) !

WORD BOX   It   doing   heroes   sound

Grammar & Writing Zone  Unit 11

10 min

 **Learn and practice.**

Verb	Present Continuous
pull	pulling
climb	am / are / is + climbing
smoke	smoking
help	helping

Change the verbs into present continuous forms.

1. They pull out the hose.

   → They [   ] [   ] out the hose.

2. They climb up the ladder.

   → They [   ] [   ] up the ladder.

Complete the sentences.

They are helping people.

1.	They	are	helping	.
2.	They	are		.
3.	They			.
4.				.

Sing A Song!

Hey ho! Hey ho! Here come the heroes.

Hey ho! Hey ho! What are they doing?

They are pulling out the hose.

They are spraying water.

They are climbing up the ladder.

Hey ho! Hey ho! Here come the heroes.

Hey ho! Hey ho! What are they doing?

They are helping people.

They are saving lives.

They are going back to rest. Hey ho!

Number the song order.

Let's Do It At Home

check box
parents
teacher

1. Listen and circle.

❶  

ⓐ ⓑ

❷  

ⓐ ⓑ

2. Read and match.

❶ The firefighter is wearing the mask.

ⓐ ⓑ ⓒ

❷ The firefighter is connecting the hose to the hydrant.

ⓐ ⓑ ⓒ

3. Unscramble the sentences.

❶ are / What / doing / they / ?

____

❷ are / They / up / the / climbing / ladder / .

____

Unit 12 — Why Do You Like Cartoons?

47

Pam: Well, I don't like cartoons. Why do you like them?

Tina: Because they are funny! How about you, Pam?

Pam: I like nature shows.

Tina: Hmm… Why do you like them?

Pam: They are interesting. I can learn many things from it.
But my favorites are news programs.

Tina: Eww, they are boring to me.

Pam: Actually, I watch them everyday.

Tina: I think you are different from me.

Role play

comedies   game shows   sports   soap dramas

 **Reading Zone!** 

Read the story and answer the questions.

> I usually watch TV before dinner.
> I like cartoons and comedies because they are funny.
> I don't like news programs and nature shows because they are boring.
> But Pam enjoys news and nature shows.
> Pam is my best friend but he is so different from me!

 **Answer the questions.**

1. What TV programs does Tina like? Circle.

    ① Comedies   ② News   ③ Nature Shows   ④ Cartoons

2. What TV programs does Pam like? Circle.

    ① Game Shows   ② News   ③ Nature Shows   ④ Dramas

3. Why does Tina like cartoons? Write.

    Because they are __________.

1. Listen and repeat. Then trace.

1. cartoons
2. nature shows
3. news
4. comedies

2. Listen and circle.

Why do you like the show?

1.

interesting

funny

2.

boring

interesting

3. Listen and fill in the blanks using the given words.

1. What ___ of TV shows do you like?

2. I ___ cartoons.

3. ___ do you like cartoons?

4. ___ they are funny.

WORD BOX   like   kind   Because   Why

Grammar & Writing Zone 

⭐ Learn and practice.

WH Question-WHY				Respond-Reason
Why do + you / I they / we + verb ~?				Because ~ .

🌀 Fill in the blanks.

1. [______] do you like news shows?

2. [______] they are interesting.

3. Why [______] you like comedies?

4. Because they are [______] .

WORD BOX   funny   Because   do   Why

✔ Complete the sentences.

> Why do you like cartoons?

1. | Why | do | you | like | | ? |

2. | Why | do | you | | | ? |

3. | Why | | | | | ? |

4. | | | | | | ? |

 Let's **Play**

Roll a die!

What kind of TV shows do you like?

Why do you like ~?

I like ~.

Because they are ~.

funny

exciting

interesting

exciting

funny

〈Tips!〉 두 팀이서 합니다. 한 팀이 What kind of TV shows do you like? 하고 물으면 상대팀 중 한 사람이 주사위를 던져서 나오는 그림에 맞게 대답합니다. 다음에는 Why do you like ~? 하고 질문하면 주사위를 던져서 그 주사위 아래 부분에 나온 단어를 이용하여 Because로 대답합니다.

Let's Do It At Home

50

1. Listen and circle.

1

Sports   Game Shows

ⓐ   ⓑ

2

interesting   boring

ⓐ   ⓑ

2. True or False? Read and circle.

A: Mary what kind of TV shows do you like?

B: I like nature shows.

A: Why do you like them?

B: Because they are interesting.

→ Mary likes nature shows because they are funny.

True	False

3. Unscramble the sentences.

1 do / kind of / What / TV shows / like / you / ?

____

2 they / are / interesting / Because / .

____

 Unit 13 — **How Tall Are You?**

51

Max: Oops!

Joe: Oh, no!

Max: I cannot reach it.

Joe: What should we do now?

Man: Hey, guys, what's the matter?
Do you need
some help?

Max: Yes, please.
We cannot
get the ball
down.

Man: Here you are!

Max&Joe: Wow! Thank you so much.

Joe: You are so tall. How tall are you?

Man: I am 2 meters tall.

Joe: Incredible! I wish I was as tall as him.

Max: Me, too!

mom

dad

brother

sister

 **Reading Zone!** 

52 **Read the story and answer the questions.**

How tall are you?

Me? I am 126cm.

Are you taller than me?

Are you shorter than me?

Today I saw a guy. He was 2 meters tall!

He is the tallest man I've ever seen.

Do you want to be as tall as him?

Now, let's measure your height!

 **Answer the questions.**

1. How tall is Joe?

   → ________________________________

2. Are you taller (or shorter) than Joe?
   Write and say it.

   → I am [   ] than Joe.

3. True or False? Circle.

   → The guy was as tall as Joe.    True | False

10 min

53

1. Listen and repeat. Then trace.

1. **meter**

2. **centimeter**

3. **taller**

4. **shorter**

2. Listen and mark it on the ruler.

3. Listen and fill in the blanks using the given words.

1. I cannot ____________ it.

2. What ____________ we do?

3. Do you need some ____________ ?

4. I am 2 meters ____________ .

WORD BOX   should   tall   reach   help

Grammar & Writing Zone  10 min

⭐ Learn and practice.

WH Questions- HOW	Answer
How tall am I?	I am ~ tall.
How tall are you / we / they?	You / We / They are ~ tall.
How tall is she / he / it?	She / He / It is ~ tall.

🌀 Read and match.

1. How tall are you? •
2. How tall is it? •
3. How tall is she? •

• ⓐ It is 1 meter tall.
• ⓑ She is 130cm tall.
• ⓒ I am 125cm tall.

✔ Complete the sentences.

> How tall are you?

1.	How	tall	are	?
2.	How	tall		?
3.	How			?
4.				?

Let's **Play**

10 min

Find the person!

How tall
are you?

____

I am

__________ cm tall.

How tall is
she/he?

____

She/He is

__________ cm tall.

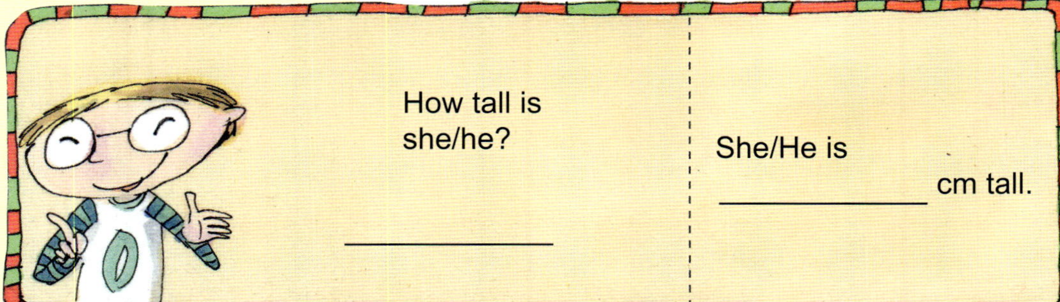

〈Tips!〉 먼저 아이들에게 I am 이라고 쓰여 있는 칸에 자신의 키를 적게 합니다. 선생님이 카드를 다 모아서 섞습니다. 아이들에게 카드를 하나씩 나누어 주고, 아이들은 돌아다니며 How tall are you?라고 물으며 그 키의 주인을 찾게 합니다. 찾으면 How tall are you?라는 란에 찾은 아이의 이름을 적습니다. 두번째 카드도 마찬가지로, She 나 He 중 하나를 고른다면 키를 씁니다. 카드를 모아서 나눈 후 그 키를 쓴 친구를 찾는 게임입니다.

Let's Do It At Home

check box	
parents	
teacher	

1. Listen and number.

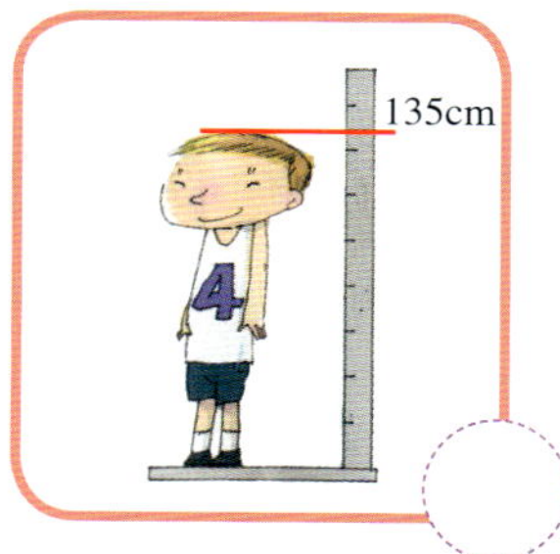

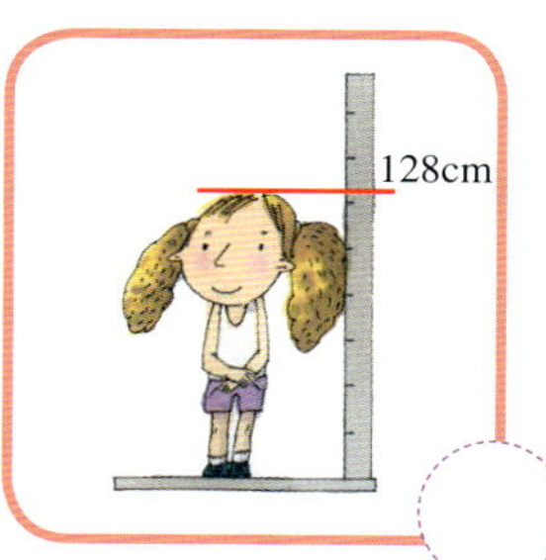

2. Read and circle.

Mark: Mary, how tall are you?

Mary: Hmm... I do not know. Let's measure my height.

Mark: Wow, you are 132cm tall. You are taller than me.

① 

② 

③ 

3. Unscramble the sentences.

① help / you / Do / some / need / ?

____

② am / I / two / tall / meters / .

____

It Must Be The Pizzaman!

10 min

DATE   /

Role play

mailman

newsboy

milkman

deliveryman

Reading **Z**one**!** 

Read the story and answer the questions.

Here is a pizza cut into 6 slices.
If there are two of you, each can have 3 slices.
But, if there are three of you, each can have 2 slices.
What if there are 4 friends?
Hmm… You can not eat it evenly.
But it doesn't matter.
Because even one slice of pizza is yummy.

Answer the questions.

1. How many pieces are there in the pizza?

    ❶ 4 pieces   ❷ 5 pieces   ❸ 6 pieces   ❹ 8 pieces

2. There are 3 friends. How many slices can each person eat according to the story?

    ❶    ❷    ❸ 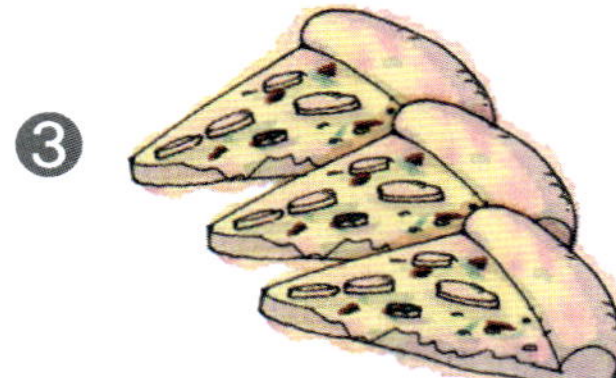

3. True or False?

    → You can eat the pizza evenly if there are 4 friends.

    | True | False |

1. Listen and repeat. Then trace.

1. **pizzaman**

2. **mailman**

3. **newsboy**

4. **milkman**

2. Listen and circle.

1.  

2.  

3. Listen and fill in the blanks using the given words.

1. ( ) is it?

2. It ( ) be the pizzaman.

3. There are six ( ).

4. I ( ) that I called him to come.

WORD BOX   must   forgot   slices   Who

Grammar & Writing Zone

★ Learn and practice.

Verb	Must - Possibility
pizzaman	It **must** be the pizzaman.
mailman	It **must** be the mailman.
milkman	It **must** be the milkman.

🌀 Read aloud and trace.

1. It **must be** the  .

2. It **must be** the  .

3. It **must be** the .

✔ Complete the sentences.

> It must be the pizzaman.

1. It | must | be | the | | .

2. It | must | be | | | .

3. It | | | | | .

4. | | | | | .

Pick up a card and answer to your friends.

the pizzaman

the mailman

the milkman

the newsboy

the delivery man

my friend

〈Tips!〉 아이들을 두 팀으로 나눕니다. 선생님이 아래 카드를 다 오린 후 빨대에 붙입니다. 그리고 책상 위에 뒤집어서 올려놓은 후 그 중 하나를 고릅니다. 아이들이 누구를 골랐는지 볼 수 없게 들고 있으면서 한 손으로 책상을 두드리며 Knock, Knock 하면, 아이들이 모두 Who is it? 하고 물어봅니다. 한 팀에 두 번씩 기회를 주고 It must be ~ 표현을 써서 답을 맞추게 합니다.

Let's Do It At Home

1. Listen and circle.

❶  

ⓐ　　　ⓑ

❷  

ⓐ　　　ⓑ

2. Read and match.

❶ It must be the mailman. •

❷ It must be the milkman. •

❸ It must be the pizza man. •

 • ⓐ

 • ⓑ

 • ⓒ

3. Unscramble and make sentences.

❶ 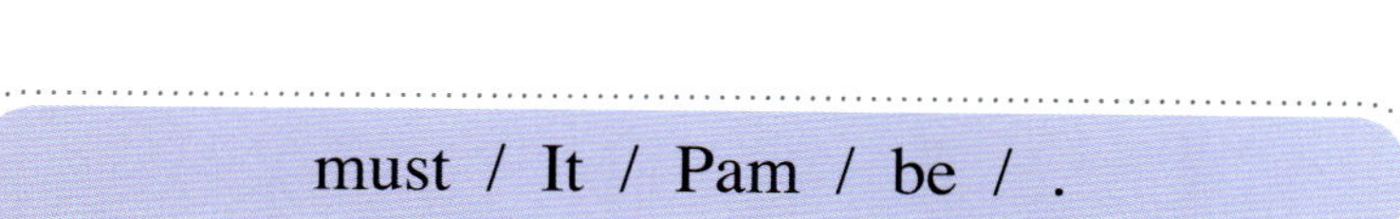

____

❷

____

How Long Does It Take To Be A Frog?

DATE /

59

1

2

3

4

5

6

Role play

to be a chick

to be a hen

to be a caterpillar

to be a butterfly

Reading Zone! 

 **Read the story and answer the questions.**

Today I saw some frog's eggs in the pond.

I wondered how long it takes for them to become tadpoles and then frogs.

Alice knew a lot about frogs.

She said it would take about 2 weeks for it to become a tadpole.

Then one or two months later, they will become adult frogs.

Wow, what an interesting thing!

 **Answer the questions.**

1. What did Max see in the pond?

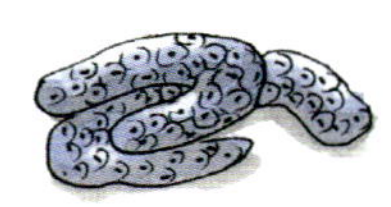    

❶ frog's eggs ❷ frog ❸ tadpole ❹ hen's eggs

2. How long does it take for the eggs to become tadpoles?

❶ 2 days ❷ 2 weeks ❸ 2 months ❹ 2 years

3. True or False?

→ It will take one year for tadpoles to become frogs. | True | False |

 **Listening Zone!** 

1. Listen and repeat. Then trace.

1. **eggs**
2. **tadpole**
3. **frog**
4. **scientist**

2. Listen and match.

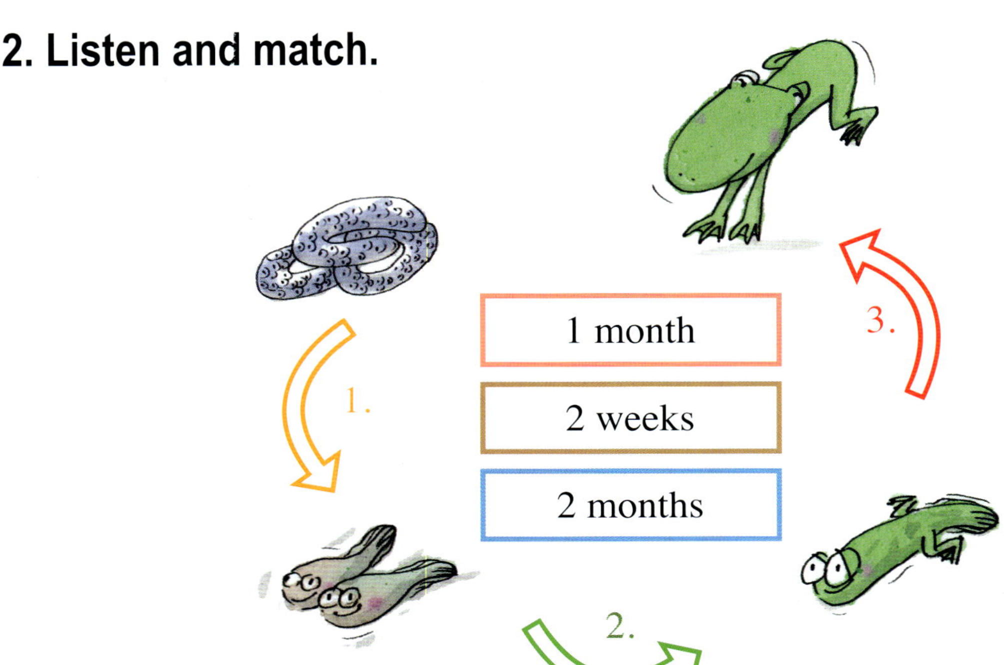

3. Listen and fill in the blanks using the given words.

1. Will they ___________ into tadpoles?

2. How ___________ does it take to be a tadpole?

3. ___________ do the legs start to grow?

4. You are like a ___________ .

WORD BOX　　long　　turn　　scientist　　When

Grammar & Writing Zone

⭐ Learn and practice.

WH Questions- HOW LONG (length-time)	Answer (length-time)
How long + does it take ~ ? will it take ~ ? → How long does it take to become a tadpole? → How long will it take to become a frog?	One hour Two weeks Three months

🌀 Fill in the blanks.

1. How long does it take for eggs to become a tadpole?

   ❶ 10 miles   ❷ 2 weeks   ❸ 5 times

2. How long will it take for eggs to become a frog?

   ❶ 3 o'clock   ❷ 2 months   ❸ at noon

✔ Complete the sentences.

> How long does it take to be tadpoles?

1.	How	long	dose	it	take	to	be		?

2.	How	long	dose	it	take		?

3.	How	long	dose		?

4.	How		?

Frog Maze!

Let's Play

10 min

You Need

pencil

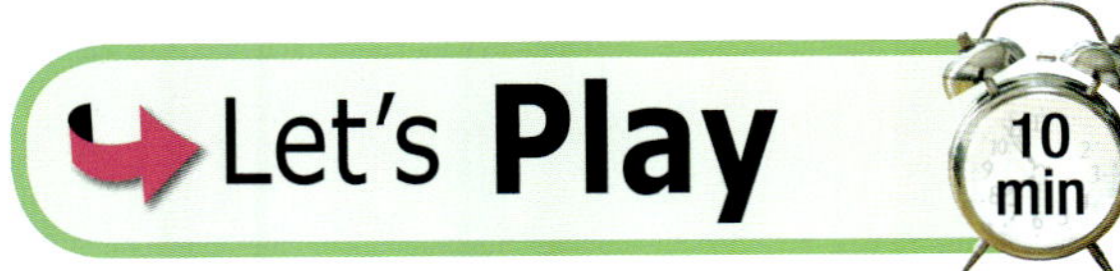

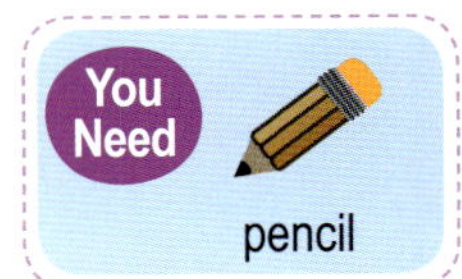

Find two sentences to escape from the maze!

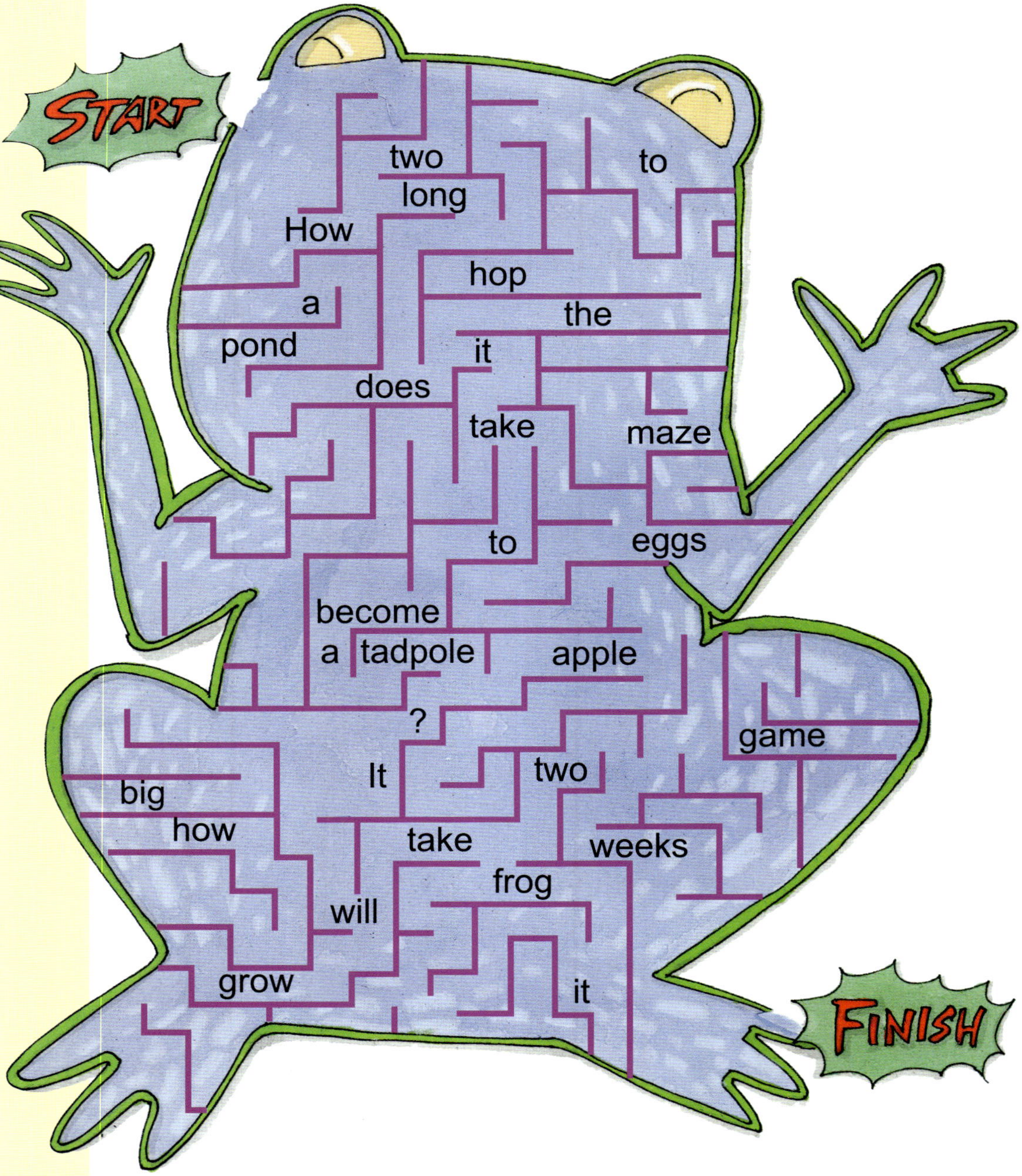

Write the two sentences.

A:

B:

〈Tips!〉 미로의 길을 찾으면 미로 길을 따라 놓여있는 단어들을 순서대로 쓰면 두 문장이 만들어 집니다.
길을 찾은 후 두 문장을 아래의 빈칸에 씁니다.

Let's Do It At Home

<table><tr><td></td><td>check box</td></tr><tr><td>parents</td><td></td></tr><tr><td>teacher</td><td></td></tr></table>

1. Listen and number in order.

ⓐ 12 days ⓑ 20 days

ⓐ 2 months ⓑ 3 months

2. Read and put the stickers. 

❶ A: How long does it take for eggs to become tadpoles?

B: 2 weeks.

❷ A: How long will it take for tadpoles to become frogs?

B: 2 months.

❶ 2 weeks ❷ 2 months

3. Unscramble the sentences.

❶ weeks / takes / It / two / about / .

____

❷ scientist / are / You / a / like / !

____

I Wish I Had A Nice Bike

DATE   /

63

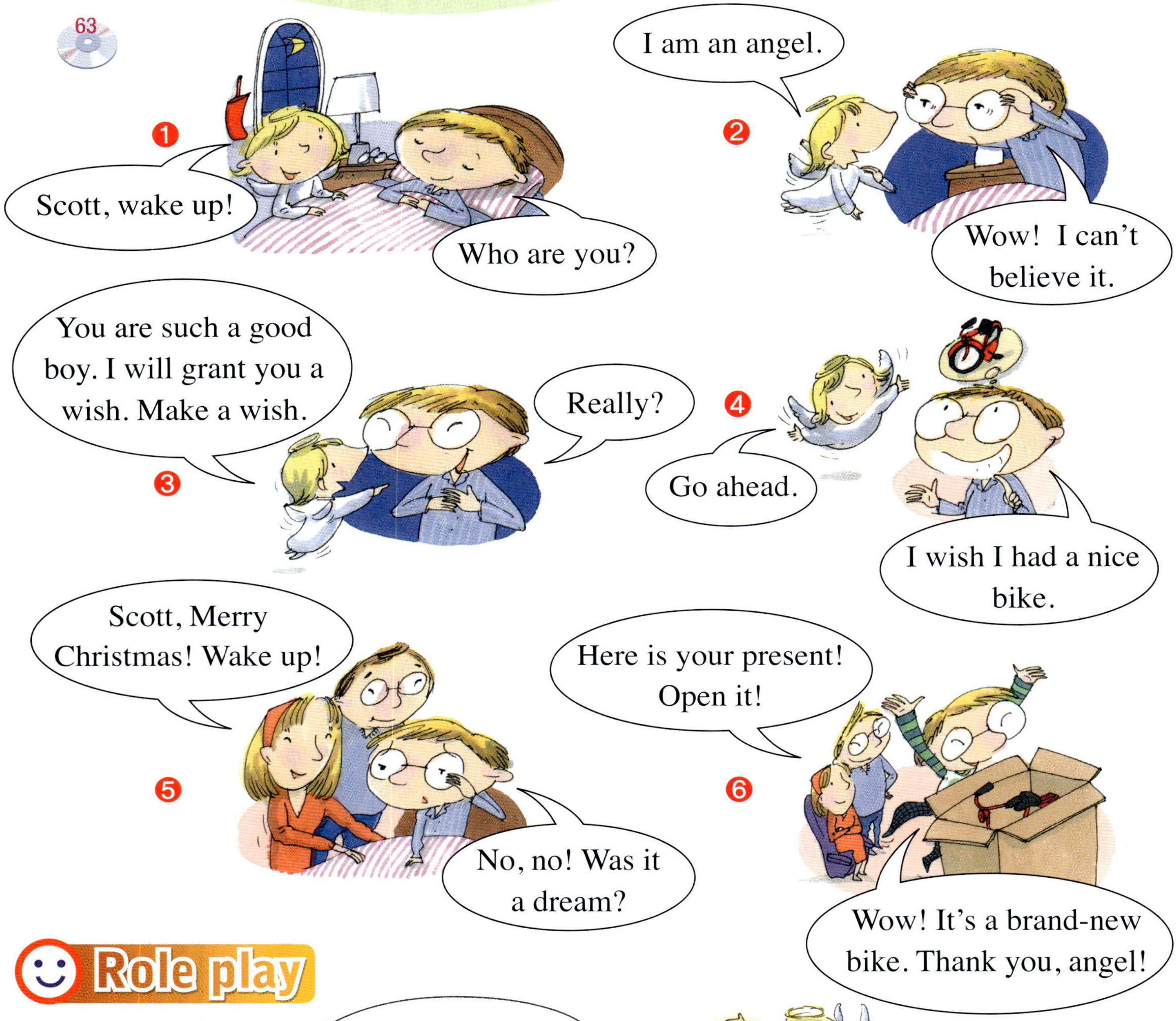

❶

❷

❸

❹

❺

❻

Role play

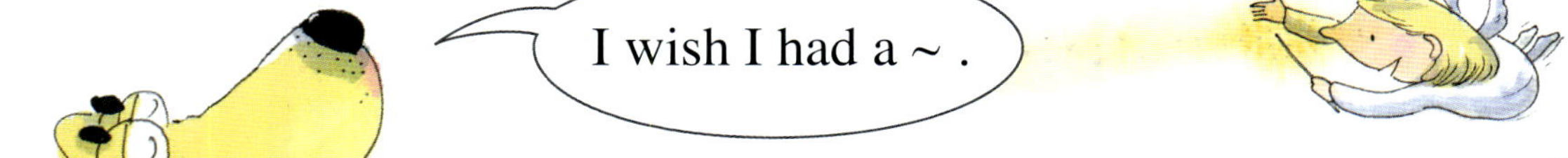

new car

new book

cell phone

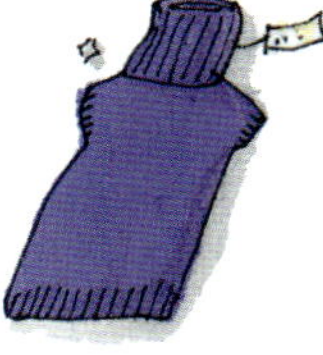

new dress

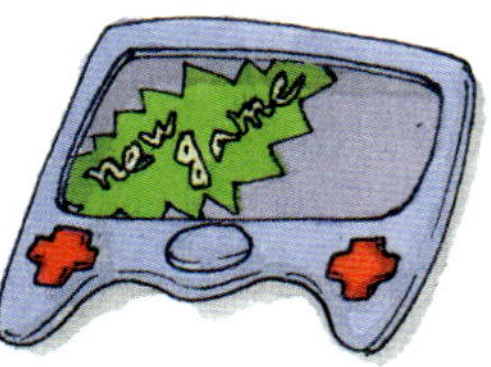

new game

Reading **Z**one**!**

 **Read the story and answer the questions.**

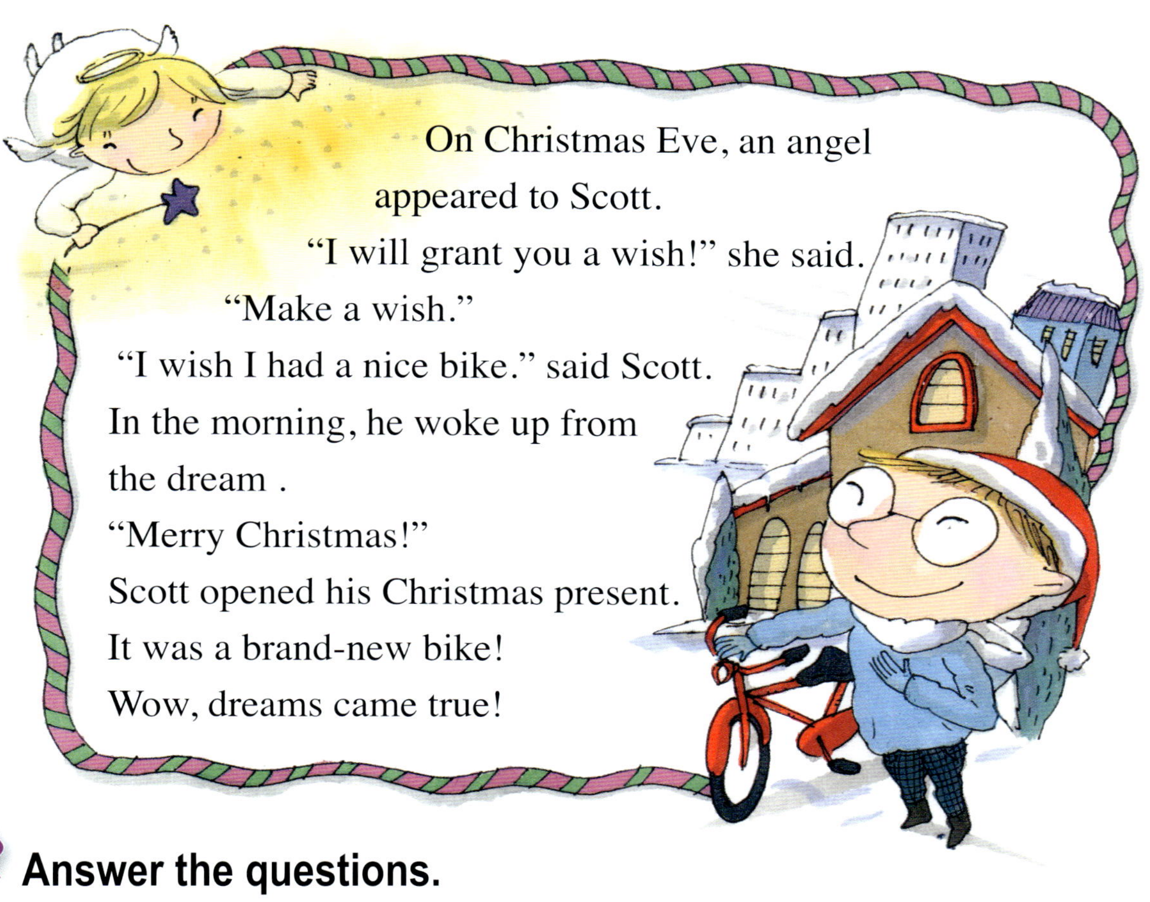

On Christmas Eve, an angel appeared to Scott.

"I will grant you a wish!" she said.

"Make a wish."

"I wish I had a nice bike." said Scott.

In the morning, he woke up from the dream .

"Merry Christmas!"

Scott opened his Christmas present.

It was a brand-new bike!

Wow, dreams came true!

Answer the questions.

1. Who appeared on Christmas Eve to Scott?

  ❶ his mom   ❷ his dad   ❸ a friend   ❹ an angel

2. Unscramble the sentence.

> **I / had / I / a / bike / wish / nice / .**

→ ____

3. True or False?

→ Scott got a bike as a Christmas present. | True | False |

1. Listen and repeat. Then trace.

1. angel

2. wish

3. Christmas

4. present

2. Listen and put the stickers on. 

1. 

2. 

3. 

4. 

3. Listen and fill in the blanks using the given words.

1. I can't ( ) it.

2. ( ) a wish!

3. I wish I ( ) a nice bike.

4. ( ) is your present.

WORD BOX   Make   had   believe   Here

 Unit **16**

 **Learn and practice.**

Conditional - I wish

		I had a bike.
I wish	+	I had a car.
		I had a dress.

Read and match.

1. I wish I had a car.   •

2. I wish I had a bike.   •

3. I wish I had a dress.   •

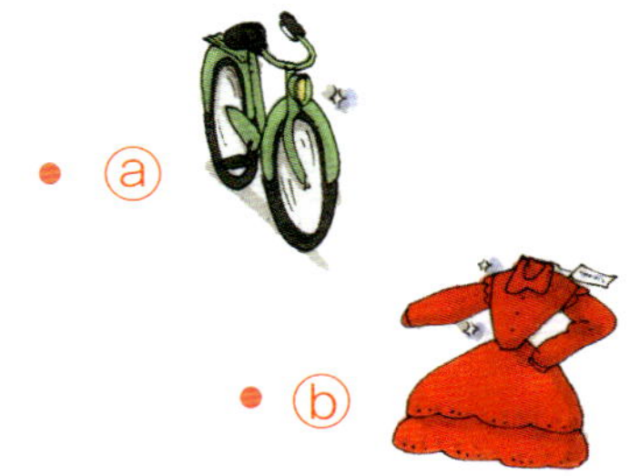

• ⓐ

• ⓑ

• ⓒ

Complete the sentences.

I wish I had a nice bike.

1. | I | wish | I | had | a | | . |

2. | I | wish | I | had | | . |

3. | I | wish | | . |

4. | | . |

Let's make a wish!

10 new car	20 new dress	30 new bike	40 new game
10 new car	20 new dress	30 new bike	40 new game
10 new car	20 new dress	30 new bike	40 new game
10 new car	20 new dress	30 new bike	40 new game

⟨Tips!⟩ 카드를 오려서 섞은 다음 셋에서 5장씩 가지고, 나머지 카드는 보이지 않게 엎어둡니다. 한 사람이 자신의 카드를 내며 'I wish I had a new bike'라고 하면 같은 색이나 같은 단어의 카드를 낼 수 있습니다. 카드의 점수가 가장 높은 사람이 카드를 모두 가져갑니다. 그 다음, 엎어둔 카드에서 각자 한 장씩 가져가고 같은 방식으로 게임합니다. 가장 많은 카드를 가진 사람이 이기는 게임입니다.

Let's Do It At Home

check box	
parents	
teacher	

1. Listen and match.

①  • • ⓐ

②  • • ⓑ

③  • • ⓒ

2. Read and circle.

A: Make a wish!

B: I wish I had a new game.

①    ②    ③ 

3. Unscramble the sentences.

① wish / a / Make / !

____

② is / Here / present / your / .

____

Test 1
Unit 1-Unit 8

SCORE OF THE TEST	
LISTENING	／ 8
READING	／ 8
WRITING	／ 4
TOTAL	／ 20

Listening Test L

 **67** 1〜4

1. 대화를 잘 듣고 알맞은 답을 고르세요.

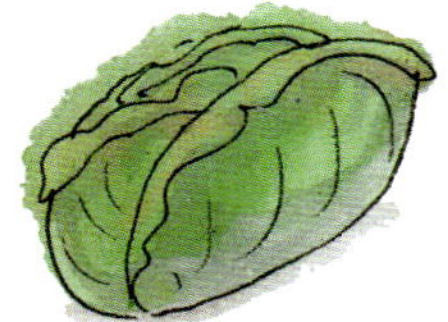

Yes	No

2. 대화를 잘 듣고 알맞은 답을 고르세요.

❶ Diego's pet store   ❷ Doctor Kim's office   ❸ Dora's pizza

3. 잘 듣고 알맞은 답을 고르세요.

his
her
mine

4. 대화를 잘 듣고 알맞은 답을 고르세요.

❶    ❷    ❸ 

 5~8

5. 대화를 잘 듣고 대화 속 두 사람이 어디를 가기로 했는지 알맞은 장소를 고르세요.

❶ 　　❷ 　　❸ 

6. 대화를 잘 듣고 소녀가 무엇을 더 자주 해야 하는지 알맞은 답을 고르세요.

❶ 　　❷ 　　❸ 

7. 대화를 잘 듣고 알맞은 답을 고르세요.

❶ 　　❷ 　　❸ 

8. 대화를 잘 듣고 소녀가 원하는 동물이 무엇인지 고르세요.

❶ 　　❷ 

Reading Test 

9. 문장을 읽고 냉장고에 없는 것에 동그라미 하세요.

> I need tomatoes, eggs and apples.
> But there are no eggs in the fridge.

❶ 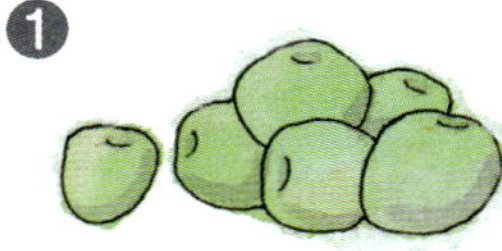　　❷ 　　❸ 

10. 대화를 읽고 알맞은 곳에 동그라미 하세요.

A: Where is Kid's toy store?
B: It is next to Doctor Kim's office.

11. 문장을 읽고 같은 뜻의 알맞은 문장과 연결하세요.

❶ My bike is nice. • • ⓐ Hers is nice.

❷ Her bike is nice. • • ⓑ Mine is nice.

12. 대화를 읽고 맞는 그림에 동그라미 하세요.

A: Is he chubby?
B: No, he is thin.

❶  ❷ 

13. 다음 문장을 읽고 알맞은 그림을 고르세요.

Let's take a picture!

❶  ❷  ❸ 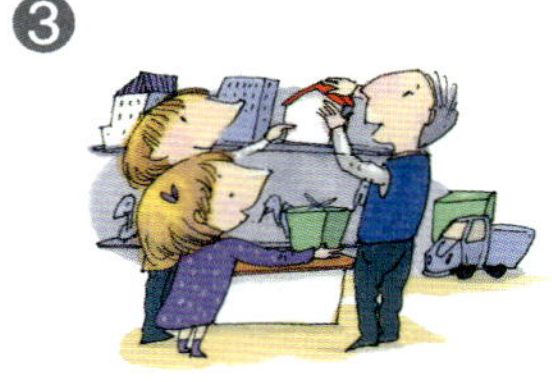

14. 그림을 보고 알맞은 문장을 고르세요.

❶ You should wash your hands.

❷ You should brush your teeth.

15. 문장을 읽고 알맞은 그림을 고르세요.

The girl is as strong as the boy.

❶  ❷  ❸ 

16. 다음 대화를 읽고 B가 원하는 동물이 무엇인지 고르세요.

A: Do you want a bird or a fish?

B: I want a fish.

 ❶    ❷

Writing Test 

17. 밑줄친 부분을 바르게 고쳐 쓰세요.

A: Mike, where are you going?

B: I am going to <u>John house</u>.

➡ _______________________________________

18. 다음 중 한 단어를 골라 빈 칸에 쓰세요.

My bike is green.

= _________________ is green.

WORD BOX His   Hers   Mine

19. 빈칸에 알맞은 말을 골라 쓰세요.

You are weak. You _________________ exercise often.

WORD BOX do   should   not

20. 그림을 보고 빈칸에 알맞은 말을 쓰세요.

WORD BOX

as - as

more - than

so - as

➡ He is ________ rich ________ her.

Test 2
Unit 9-Unit 16

SCORE OF THE TEST		
LISTENING	/	8
READING	/	8
WRITING	/	4
TOTAL	/	20

Listening Test L

 **69** 1~4

1. 대화를 잘 듣고 알맞은 답을 고르세요.

❶ grease   ❷ smoke   ❸ mash

2. 대화를 잘 듣고 알맞은 방향을 고르세요.

❶ east   ❷ south   ❸ north

3. 대화를 잘 듣고 알맞은 답을 고르세요.

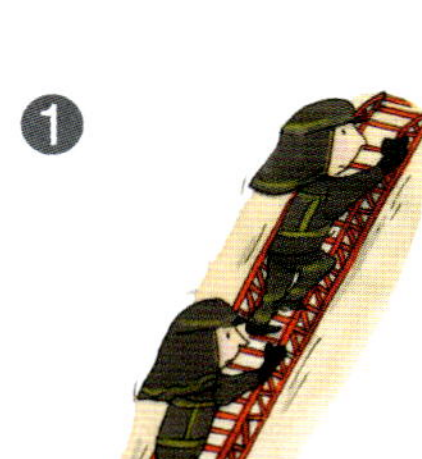  

4. 잘 듣고 알맞은 답을 고르세요.

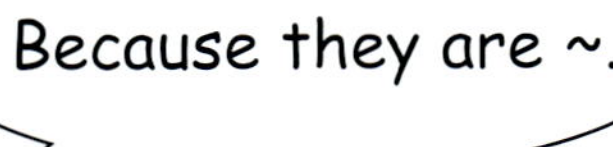

❶ exciting

❷ funny

❸ boring

70 5~8

5. 잘 듣고 John의 키가 몇인지 고르세요.

 ❶    ❷    ❸

120cm   126cm   131cm

6. 대화를 잘 듣고 밖에 누가 찾아왔는지 고르세요.

 ❶    ❷    ❸

7. 대화를 잘 듣고 알맞은 답을 고르세요.

❶ 2 weeks

❷ 1 month

❸ 2 months

8. 대화를 잘 듣고 알맞은 답을 고르세요.

 ❶   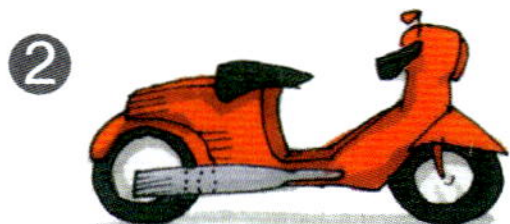 ❷    ❸

Reading Test **R**

9. 그림을 보고 빈칸에 알맞은 답을 고르세요.

Q: Who will help me _______________ the pan?

❶ grease

❷ beat

❸ mash

10. 잘 보고 알맞은 답을 고르세요.

A: What does the map say?
B: It says…

11. 그림을 보고 알맞은 답을 고르세요.

What are they doing?

❶ They are helping people.
❷ They are spraying water.
❸ They are climbing up the ladder.

12. 문장을 읽고 True 또는 False에 동그라미 하세요.

Mary: I like nature shows.
Paul: Why do you like them?
Mary: Because they are interesting.

True / False

➡ Mary likes nature shows because they are funny.

13. 대화를 읽고 알맞은 답을 고르세요.

A: Suzy, how tall are you?
B: I am One hundred thirty two centimeters tall.

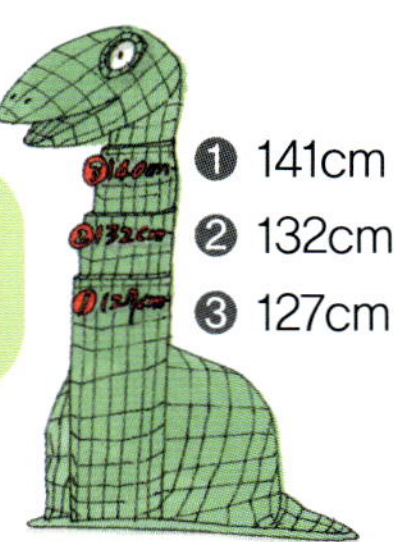

14. 그림을 보고 맞는 단어에 동그라미 하세요.

A: Who is it?
B: It must be the mailman / milkman .

15. 그림을 보고 알맞은 답을 고르세요.

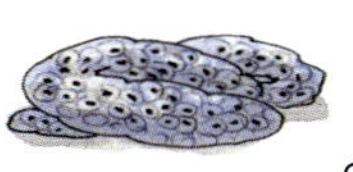

Q: How long does it take eggs to become tadpoles?

❶ 2 days   ❷ 2 weeks   ❸ 2 months

16. 대화를 읽고 알맞은 답을
    고르세요.

A: Make a wish!
B: I wish I had a new book.

❶  ❷  ❸ 

Writing Test 

17. 단어를 올바른 순서로 써보세요.

A: I am going to make a cake.
   will / Who / me / help make a cake?

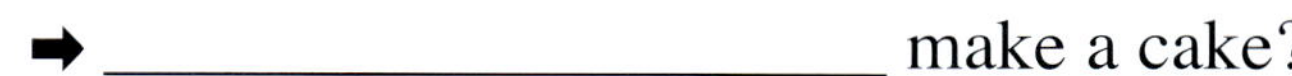

➡ _________________________ make a cake?

18. 색칠된 부분을 바르게 고쳐
    쓰세요.

A: What are they doing?
B: They are pull out the hose.

➡ They _________________________ the hose.

19. 빈칸에 들어갈 단어를 쓰세요.

A: Who is it?
B: It ________ be the pizzaman.

WORD BOX   had   going   is   must

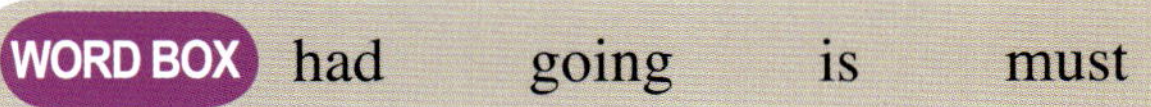

20. 빈칸에 알맞은 단어를 쓰세요.

A: Make a wish!
B: I ________ I ________ a nice bike.

WORD BOX   must   wish   as   had

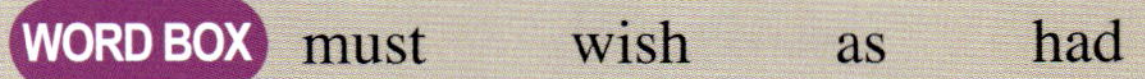

Name :

Final Test
Unit 1-Unit 16

Listening Test **L**

SCORE OF THE TEST		
LISTENING	/	8
READING	/	8
WRITING	/	4
TOTAL	/	20

 **71** 1~4

1. 대화를 잘 듣고 없는 것에 동그라미 하세요.

① ② ③

2. 잘 듣고 자전거의 주인을 찾아주세요.

①   •   • ⓐ hers

②   •   • ⓑ mine

3. 잘 듣고 빈칸에 들어갈 알맞은 단어에 동그라미 하세요.

❶ Must   ❷ Who   ❸ Should   ❹ Let's

4. 잘 듣고 내용과 일치하는 그림을 고르세요.

① ② ③

Final Test

5. 잘 듣고 들은 순서대로 그림에
   번호를 쓰세요.

6. 잘 듣고 소방관들이 무엇을 하고
   있는지 알맞은 답을 고르세요.

❶  ❷  ❸ 

7. 잘 듣고 알맞게 연결하세요.

❶ ·　　　　　· ⓐ 131 cm

❷ ·　　　　　· ⓑ 135cm

8. 대화를 듣고 알맞은 답을
   고르세요.

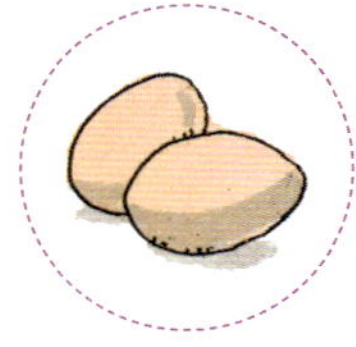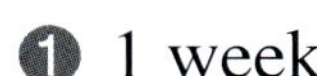 → 

❶ 1 week　　❷ 2 weeks　　❸ 3 weeks

Reading Test R

9. 문장을 읽고 알맞은 번호를
   고르세요.

Mike's house is between Dora's pizza and Kid's toy store.

| Diego's pet store | ❶ | Dora's pizza | | Dora's pizza | ❷ | kid's toy store |

| kid's toy store |  | ❸ |  | Dora's pizza | ❹ |

Final Test

10. 잘 읽고 알맞은 그림을
고르세요.

A: Is Bob skinny?
B: No, he is chubby.
A: Is he short?
B: Yes, he is short.

 ❶  ❷  ❸

11. 대화를 읽고 빈칸에 들어갈
알맞은 단어를 고르세요.

A: I wake up late and I am often late for school.
B: You ____________ wake up earlier.

❶ should　　❷ as　　❸ are　　❹ Let's

12. 대화를 잘 읽고 B가 원하는
동물을 고르세요.

A: Do you want a goldfish
　　or a rabbit?
B: I want a goldfish.

 ❶  ❷

13. 잘 읽고 True 또는 False에
동그라미 하세요.

What does it say?
➡ It says, "climb up the mountain."

True / False

14. 빈칸에 들어갈 알맞은 단어를
고르세요.

A: Why do you like the news?
B: ____________ it is interesting.

❶ Must　　❷ How　　❸ Because　　❹ Will

15. 잘 읽고 알맞은 답을 고르세요.

A: Who is it?
B: It must be the paperboy.

 ❶　❷　❸ 

Final Test

A: Make a wish!
B: ________________________________

16. 잘 읽고 빈칸에 들어갈 문장을 고르세요.

❶ It must be the pizzaman!
❷ You should brush your teeth.
❸ I wish I had a new dress.

Writing Test 

17. 주어진 단어를 이용하여 문장을 만들어 보세요

A: Where is the lettuce?
B: is / There / lettuce / no / .

➡ ________________________________

18. 틀린 곳을 찾아 바르게 쓰세요.

He is as brave than the man.
    ❶   ❷   ❸   ❹

➡ ____________________

19. 빈칸에 들어갈 알맞은 말을 쓰세요.

A: __________ do you like comedies?
B: Because they are funny.

WORD BOX   Who   What   Why   How

20. 빈칸에 공통으로 들어갈 말을 쓰세요.

❶ ____________ tall are you?

❷ ____________ long does it take to become frogs?

WORD BOX   Who   What   Why   How

Unit 1 — There Is No Lettuce

New Vocabularies

sandwich	sandwich
lettuce	lettuce
cabbage	cabbage
peach	peach
bean	bean
sprouts	sprouts
raisins	raisins
radish	radish
hungry	hungry

New Expressions

There are no eggs.

There is no lettuce.

Is there cheese in the fridge?

Unit 2   I Am Going To Mike's House

<table>
<tr><td></td><td colspan="2">check box</td></tr>
<tr><td>parents</td><td></td></tr>
<tr><td>teacher</td><td></td></tr>
</table>

New Vocabularies

pet store — pet store

school — school

auto shop — auto shop

toy store — toy store

restaurant — restaurant

next to — next to

between — between

ask — ask

borrow — borrow

New Expressions

I am going to Mike's house.

Doctor Kim's office is next to my house.

Where is Dora's pizza?

Unit 3 — It Is Mine

	check box
parents	
teacher	

New Vocabularies

scooter	scooter
toy car	toy car
skateboard	skateboard
mine	mine
ours	ours
yours	yours
his	his
hers	hers
theirs	theirs
brand-new	brand-new

New Expressions

Whose bike is this?

That's mine.

His is brand-new.

Unit 4 — Is He Tall?

	check box
parents	
teacher	

tall	tall
short	short
fat	fat
stout	stout
chubby	chubby
thin	thin
slim	slim
skinny	skinny

Am I thin?

Is he stout?

Are they tall?

Let's Go To The Dinosaur Museum!

	check box
parents	
teacher	

New Vocabularies

dinosaur

museum

buy a ticket

ask to the guide

tour the museum

go see the fossils

New Expressions

Let's go to the museum.

Let's take a picture.

Let's use the map.

You Should Stop Eating Too Much Candy

	check box
parents	
teacher	

cavities

toothache

exercise

eat vegetable

get up early

take a shower daily

wash hands often

New Expressions

You should take a shower.

You should brush your teeth often.

You should wash your hands.

Unit 7 — I Am As Brave As Him

	check box
parents	
teacher	

clever

beautiful

rich

thin

fast

brave

strong

as ~ as

I am as strong as him.

He is as tall as I.

She is as brave as you.

 Unit 8 — Do You Want A Pet Or A Toy?

	check box
parents	
teacher	

New Vocabularies

turtle	turtle
goldfish	goldfish
hamster	hamster
rabbit	rabbit
parrot	parrot
prepare	prepare
repeat	repeat

New Expressions

Do you want a pet or a toy?

Do you want a dog or a cat?

Do you want a parrot or a parakeet?

Unit 9 — Who Will Help Me Bake A Cake?

	check box
parents	
teacher	

New Vocabularies

pour the water

sift the flour

frost the cake

cool the cookies

beat the mix

mash the bananas

grease the pan

New Expressions

Who will help me bake a cake?

Who will help me make some cookies?

Who will help me mash the bananas?

Unit 10 · What Does It Say?

	check box
parents	
teacher	

left	wake up
right	hear
north	
west	
south	
east	
treasure	
run away	
step	

What does it say?

What does she say?

It says, "Five steps to the west."

Unit 11 They Are Helping People

	check box
parents	
teacher	

wear masks and helmets   wear masks and helmets

connect the hose to the hydrant

connect the hose to the hydrant

spray water   spray water

save   save   help   help

firefighter   firefighter

die   die

hero   hero

pull out   pull out

They are pulling out the hose.

They are climbing up the ladder.

They are helping people.

Unit 12 — Why Do You Like Cartoons?

	check box
parents	
teacher	

New Vocabularies

comedies	comedies
game shows	game shows
sports	sports
soap dramas	soap dramas
cartoons	cartoons
news programs	news programs
nature shows	nature shows
learn	learn
different	different

New Expressions

Why do you like news shows?

Because they are interesting.

Why do you like comedies?

<table>
<tr><td></td><td colspan="2" align="center">check box</td></tr>
<tr><td>parents</td><td></td></tr>
<tr><td>teacher</td><td></td></tr>
</table>

Unit 13 — How Tall Are You?

New Vocabularies

reach	reach
incredible	incredible
wish	wish
taller	taller
shorter	tallest
tallest	height
measure	measure
height	shorter
meter	meter

centimeter centimeter

New Expressions

How tall are you?

I am 124 cm tall.

How tall is she?

Express Yourself

 Unit 14 — It Must Be The Pizzaman!

	check box
parents	
teacher	

New Vocabularies

mailman	mailman
newsboy	newsboy
milkman	milkman
deliveryman	deliveryman
slice	slice
evenly	evenly
forget	forget
call	call
check	check

New Expressions

It must be the pizzaman.

It must be the mailman.

It must be the milkman.

Unit 15 — How Long Does It Take To Be A Frog?

	check box
parents	
teacher	

New Vocabularies

chick	chick
hen	hen
caterpillar	caterpillar
butterfly	butterfly
scientist	scientist
adult frog	adult frog
tadpole	tadpole
wonder	wonder
become	become

New Expressions

How long does it take to be tadpoles?

How long will it take to become a frog?

You are like a scientist.

 Unit 16 | I Wish I Had A Nice Bike

	check box
parents	
teacher	

New Vocabularies

angel

grant

make a wish

go ahead

appear

New Expressions

Make a wish!

I wish I had a car.

I wish I had a dress.

Answers

Unit 1

Page 5 Reading Zone

1. ③   2. ①   3. False

Page 6 Listening Zone

2. 1. ② 2. ①   3. 1) anything 2) There 3) Where 4) no

Page 7 Grammar & Writing Zone

1. are no 2. is no

Page 8 Let's Play

eggs, ham, cabbage, radish, raisins, peach

Page 9 Let's Do It At Home

1. 1) X 2) X   2. No
3. 1) I can make sandwiches. 2) There are no more eggs.

Unit 2

Page 11 Reading Zone

1. ②   2. 1) True 2) False

Page 12 Listening Zone

2. Daddy's auto shop – Alice's house – Kid's toy store
   Dora's pizza – Diego's pet store – Bob's house
3. 1) going 2) Mike's 3) borrowed 4) next

Page 13 Grammar & Writing Zone

1. Dora's pizza
2. Mike's house
3. Diego's pet store

Page 15 Let's Do It At Home!

1. 1) a 2) b   2. 4
3. 1) Is that Mike's book?
   2) His house is next to Dora's pizza.

Unit 3

Page 17 Reading Zone

1. Yes 2. ③ 3. His

Page 18 Listening Zone

2. 1) c 2) b 3) a
3. 1) Whose 2) Mine 3) Nicer 4) his

Page 19 Grammar & Writing Zone

1. Mine 2. Hers 3. His

Page 21 Let's Do It At Home!

1. 1) a 2) b   2. 1) c 2) a 3) b
3. 1. It is mine.   2. His is brand–new.

Unit 4

Page 23 Reading Zone

1. ② 2. ① 3. ①, ④

Page 24 Listening Zone

2. 1) V 2) X   3. 1) friend 2) Is 3) thin 4) blond

Page 25 Grammar & Writing Zone

1. Am I thin?
2. Is he tall?
3. Are you stout?

Page 27 Let's Do It At Home!

1. 3   2. 1) b 2) a
3. 1) Is he tall?   2) He is a little chubby.

Unit 5

Page 29 Reading Zone

1. ③
2. 1) Let's go to the museum!
   2) Let's take a picture!
   3) Let's come back again!

Page 30 Listening Zone

2. 4–2–1–3
3. 1) Let's 2) Idea 3) Dinosaur
   4) picture

Page 31 Grammar & Writing Zone

1. ② 2. ③

Page 32 Let's Play →

Page 33 Let's Do It At Home!

1. 1) c 2) b   2. 1) c 2) a 3) b
3. 1) Let's take a picture!   2) Let's use the map!

Unit 6

Page 35 Reading Zone

1. 2   2. 1) stop 2) brush

Page 36 Listening Zone

2. 2–1–3–4
3. 1) matter 2) cavities 3) should 4) brush

Page 37 Grammar & Writing Zone

1. 2 2. 1

Page 39 Let's Do It At Home!

1. 1) a 2) b   2. 1) wash 2) get
3. 1) You should exercise often.
   2) You should wash your hands.

Unit 7

Page 41 Reading Zone

1. 2, 4   2. as brave as

Page 42 Listening Zone

2. 1) 2 2) 1   3. 1) Brave 2) as 3) strong 4) watch

Page 43 Grammar & Writing Zone

1. as strong as   2. as tall as

Page 44 Let's Play →

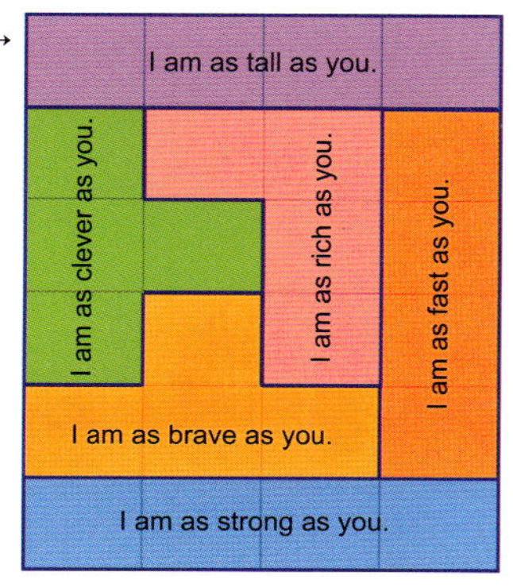

Page 45 Let's Do It At Home!

1. 2–3–1   2. 1) b 2) c 3) a   2) woman / She
3. 1) He is so brave.
   2) I am as strong as him.

Unit 8

Page 47 Reading Zone

1. ③ 2. ② 3. False

Page 48 Listening Zone

2. 1) b 2) b
3. 1) present 2) neither 3) fish 4) parakeet

Page 49 Grammar & Writing Zone

1. a turtle or a rabbit   2. a hamster or a goldfish

Page 51 Let's Do It At Home!

1. 1) c 2) a 3) b   2. 2
3. 1) I want a pet.   2) Do you want a dog or a cat?

Unit 9

Page 53 Reading Zone

1. ① 2. help / make 3. ③

Page 54 Listening Zone

2. 1) Who will help me grease the pan?
   2) Who will help me mash the bananas?
   3) Who will help me pour the water?
3. 1. Who 2. Not 3. Mash 4. myself

Page 55 Grammar & Writing Zone

1. Who 2. will 3. help

Page 56 Let's Play

1. Who will help me make the cake?
2. Who will help me bake some cookies?
3. Who will help me mash the bananas?
4. Who will help me grease the pan?
5. Who will help me beat the cake mix and bananas?

Page 57 Let's Do It At Home!

1. 1) b 2) a   2. 1) grease 2) bake
3. 1) I have to do my homework.
   2) You did not help me make the cake.

Answers

Unit 10

Page 59 Reading Zone

1. 1) sail 2) climb   2. 3–2–1

Page 60 Listening Zone

2. 1) 2 2) 3   3. 1) What 2) says 3) steps 4) Dig

Page 61 Grammar & Writing Zone

1. What does it say?

2. What does she say?

3. What does he say?

Page 63 Let's Do It At Home!

1. 1) north 2) east 3) south   2. 1

3. 1) What does it say?   2) (It says) ten steps to the right.

Unit 11

Page 65

Reading Zone

1. 1) False 2) True   2. ① ② ④

Page 66

Listening Zone

2. 4–2–1–3   3. 1) sound 2) It 3) doing 4) heroes

Page 67

Grammar & Writing Zone

1. are pulling 2. are climbing

Page 68

let's Play

1–5–2–3–4

Page 69

Let's Do It At Home!

1. 1) b 2) a   2. 1) c 2) b

3. 1) What are they doing?

   2) They are climbing up the ladder.

Unit 12

Page 71 Reading Zone

1) ① 4 2) ② ③ 3. funny

Page 72 Listening Zone

2. 1) funny 2) interesting

3. 1) kind 2) like 3) Why 4) Because

Page 73 Grammar & Writing Zone

1. Why 2. Because 3. do 4. funny

Page 75 Let's Do It At Home!

1. 1) b 2) a   2. False

3. 1) What kind of TV shows do you like?

   2) Because they are interesting.

Unit 13

Page 77 Reading Zone

1. He is 126cm (tall).   2. taller or shorter   3. False

Page 78 Listening Zone

여자아이: 1m 25cm   남자 아이: 1m 32cm

3. 1) reach   2) should 3) Help   4) tall

Page 79 Grammar & Writing Zone

1. c 2. a 3. b

Page 81

Let's Do It At Home!

1. 3–1–2   2. 2

3. 1) Do you need some help?   2) I am two meters tall.

Unit 14

Page 83 Reading Zone

1. ③ 2. ② 3. False

Page 84 Listening Zone

2. 1) ① 2) ③   3. 1) Who 2) must 3) slices 4) forgot

Page 87 Let's Do It At Home!

1. 1) a 2) b   2. 1) c 2) a 3) b

3. 1) Who is it?   2) It must be Pam.

Unit 15

Page 89 Reading Zone

1. ① 2. ② 3. False

Page 90 Listening Zone

2. 1) 2 weeks 2) 1 month 3) 2 months

3. 1) turn 2) long 3) When 4) scientist

Page 91 Grammar & Writing Zone

1. 2 2. 2

Page 92 Let's Play

A: How long does it take to become a tadpole?

B: It will take two weeks.

Page 92 Let's Play

turn on, turn off, chat, send

Page 93 Let's Do It At Home!

1. 1) a 2) a

2.   

3. 1) It takes about two weeks.   2) You are like a scientist!

Unit 16

Page 95 Reading Zone

1. 4

2. I wish I had a nice bike.

3. True

Page 96 Listening Zone

2. 1)  2)  3) 4) 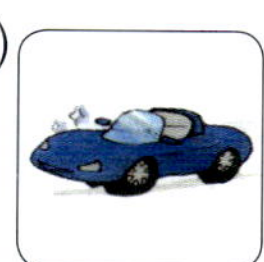

3. 1) believe 2) Make 3) had 4) Here

Page 97 Grammar & Writing Zone

1. c 2. a 3. b

Page 99 Let's Do It At Home!

1. 1) c 2) a 3) b

2. b

3. 1) Make a wish!

   2) Here is your present.

Test 1 (Unit 1-Unit 8)

Page 100

Listening Test

1. No 2. ③ 3. Mine 4. ③ 5. ② 6. ① 7. ③ 8. ①

Reading Test

9. ③ 10. ②

11. 1) b. Mine is nice. 2) a. Hers is nice.   12. 

13. ② 14. ① 15. ①

16. ②

Writing Test

17. John's house 18. Mine

19. should 20. as as

Test 2 (Unit 9-Unit 16)

Page 104

Listening Test

1. ③ 2. ② 3. ① 4. ② 5. ② 6. ① 7. ③ 8. ③

Reading Test

9. ① 10. ③ 11. ② 12. False 13. ② 14. milkman 15. ②

16. ③

Writing Test

17. Who will help me

18. are pulling out

19. must

20. wish/had

Final Test(Unit 1-Unit 16)

Page 108

Listening Test

1. ③ 2. 1) b 2) a 3. ④ 4. ③ 5. ②, ①, ③

6. 1 7. 1) b 2) a 8. 3

Reading Test

9. ② 10. ② 11. ①

12. ① 

13. False 14. ③ 15. ① 16. ③

Writing Test

17. There is no lettuce.

18. ④ as 19. Why 20. How

First Printing 2011.03.20
Author : Samuel Lee / Chanam Kim
Supervisor : LLS English Research Center
Publisher : Kiseon Lee
Publishing Company: JPLUS
467-30 Mangwon-dong, Mapo-gu, Seoul, Korea
Telephone : 02-332-8320
Fax : 02-332-8321
Homepage : www.jplus114.com

Registration Number : 10-1680
Registration Date : 1998.12.09
ISBN 978-89-94632-18-6(64740)
ISBN 978-89-94632-10-0(set)